A Masterful Retreat
The Story of The 7th Division's Retreat
Across Eastern Kentucky
from Sept. 17 - Oct. 3, 1862

by Lewis D. Nicholls

A Masterful Retreat
The Story of The 7th Division's Retreat Across Eastern Kentucky
from Sept. 17 - Oct. 3, 1862
© Copyright 2006 by Lewis D. Nicholls

ISBN # 0-9776554-0-7
Library of Congress Control Number: 2006921502

Printed in the United States of America
Avant Garde Publishing

Acknowledgments

As an active Kentucky Circuit judge, I am exposed to the rigors and stress of the courtroom on a daily basis. To alleviate these demands, I decided to write this book as an escape from the pressure of the job. I could not have picked a better subject. As a young boy I wondered about this Civil War event because of the small part that my hometown, Greenup, Kentucky played in it. So, with no experience in writing a book, performing Civil War research, or possessing even the remotest idea of how to proceed, off I embarked on a project that proved to not only be a stress reliever, but also a lot of fun.

I would like to thank my wife, Barb, for her encouragement and support during this project. She endured reenactment Civil War trips to Pomeroy, Ohio, and Cumberland Gap, Kentucky that bored her to tears. Yet, because she loved me, she was willing to go off on these weekend excursions so I could chase my dream. Barb, a college English teacher, proofread my manuscript on many occasions giving helpful suggestions along the way. I am forever indebted to her for her emotional and professional assistance.

I would also like to thank my publisher, Jenny Pemberton, for her encouragement and patience. I insisted on change after change and she cheerfully made each one never complaining. Also, her professional assistance and encouragement made this project pure enjoyment for me.

I would be remiss if I didn't thank my mother, Molly Nicholls. She encouraged me to chase my dream of writing this book and insisted that she would buy the first copy, even though I assured her that I wanted her to have it as a gift.

Last, I want to thank my father, the late Lewis H. (Pete) Nicholls, who gave me my love of history. It is to his memory that I dedicate this book.

Table of Contents

INTRODUCTION

In front of the courthouse in Greenup, Kentucky is an historical marker that reads:

Masterful Retreat

USA Brig. Gen. George W. Morgan with 8000 men reached here Oct. 3, 1862 on way to Camp Dennison, Ohio, after retreating over 200 miles from Cumberland Gap in sixteen days harassed by CSA Morgan's Raiders. USA forces had held Gap but Confederate operations based in Barbourville, 24 miles north of Gap, had cut off Union supplies and made retreat necessary.

As a young boy growing up in Greenup, I became enthralled with the "Masterful Retreat." I wondered who these men were and what hardships they endured to reach Greenup. As I became older, I did my best to find a book on the subject. To my amazement, there were no books that fully described this event. All I could find was a reference here and there alluding to the withdrawal.

During my research, I located a book written by Doctor B. F. Stevenson who was a physician with the 22nd Kentucky Infantry Regiment that participated in the famous retreat. The book is a collection of letters to his wife and friends about his exploits. On October 19, 1862, he penned a letter to Mr. Erastus Tousey in which, after some sober reflection, he commented on the significance of their Cumberland Gap expedition. In it he said,

The papers of the day have given to the public all the details of our march from Cumberland Gap to the Ohio River, that it would be proper to expose at present, but I think there is a history of the expedition yet to be written which will change the opinions of the world as to its importance, and

the policy on which it was based. That it has failed in its original design is now manifest to all; and the causes leading to that failure when they come to be investigated, will, I think, vindicate the propriety of Gen. Morgan's action.

Cumberland Gap is located in Bell County, Kentucky, along the Wilderness Road made famous by Daniel Boone as the pioneer gateway into the Mississippi and Ohio basins. Both the Union and Confederate military commands recognized that it represented the gateway into eastern Tennessee for the Union, or into Kentucky for the Confederacy. Both sides expended massive efforts to control this important pass. However, both sides failed to understand the diminished tactical importance of the Gap because of the lack of good roads to it and a flawed military doctrine that called for holding onto geographic locations instead of closing with and destroying the enemy.

Brig. Gen. George W. Morgan commanded the Union's 7th Division, comprised of approximately 10,000 soldiers. It was one of seven divisions that comprised the Army of the Ohio commanded by General Don Carlos Buell. On June 17, 1862, the 7th Division occupied Cumberland Gap after Confederate soldiers had abandoned it just hours earlier. General Morgan spent the rest of the summer trying to strengthen his defenses and build up his supplies.

During August 1862 Confederate General Kirby Smith invaded Kentucky through two adjacent passes to Cumberland Gap and took the town of Barbourville, Kentucky 25 miles north of the Gap. General Smith's invasion was part of a coordinated effort by Confederate General Braxton Bragg who invaded Kentucky through the western part of the state. Together they had a combined Confederate army of approximately 25,000 soldiers. By early September 1862, General Morgan's 7th Division was without adequate supplies to last even another month due to the poor roads. As a result of the invasion, General Morgan was cut off from his supply base in central Kentucky.

General George Morgan surveyed his situation and, after consultation with other key officers of his command, decided to abandon Cumberland Gap before he lost the entire Division. General Morgan considered taking the Mt. Sterling-Pound Gap road to Mt. Sterling, Kentucky. This was the only road leading out of eastern Kentucky into central Kentucky. Unfortunately, Confederate General Humphrey Marshall, a native Kentuckian, waited at Mt. Sterling with 3,000 troops to block General Morgan's withdrawal. Meanwhile Confederate General Carter L. Stevenson with approximately 10,000 troops positioned on the south side of Cumberland Gap was poised to attack Morgan from the south. Faced with these dire circumstances, on September 17, 1862, General Morgan led the 7th Division north and headed for the Ohio River through two hundred miles of eastern Kentucky wilderness. General Morgan's decision to move his Division through eastern Kentucky was a bold one because the roads were practically impassable for an army of this size. The men of the 7th Division had little food to eat, and the route chosen provided little prospect of finding food along the way.

General Morgan's troops marched through eastern Kentucky while being harassed by approximately 900 Confederate cavalry under the command of Col. John Hunt Morgan. The Confederates blocked the Union's path by ambushing them along the way and blocking the route with trees and rocks. Additionally, a terrible drought occurred during the summer of 1862 causing the Union army to suffer from extreme thirst.

On October 3, 1862, the 7th Division reached the small town of Greenupsburg, present day Greenup, Kentucky, on the banks of the Ohio River. They crossed the Ohio River into Union territory, thus saving the 7th Division from annihilation. The 7th Division lost only 80 men during the march; however, they inflicted 582 casualties on the Confederates during their occupation of Cumberland Gap.

In this book I have recorded the struggles of the 7th Division during the 1862 Cumberland Gap campaign. I have also examined Kentucky in the early years of the Civil War leading up to the occupation of and withdrawal from the Gap, and I have considered the Union withdrawal from both the Northern and Southern perspectives.

After the retreat, Morgan received criticism from General Halleck, Chief of Staff, for abandoning Cumberland Gap. Morgan even had to defend his decision to abandon the Gap before a military tribunal. General Morgan was simply ordered to take and defend Cumberland Gap; he did not select the Gap as an objective. The Union high command's decision to station the 7th Division at Cumberland Gap proved to be unwise because the Confederate armies invaded Kentucky through the adjacent gaps of Rogers and Big Stone Mountain, bypassing Cumberland Gap.

The U.S. Army today recognizes nine principles of war, and I have analyzed Union General George Washington Morgan's tactical decisions from the standpoint of these nine principles. I have also examined General George Morgan's leadership skills and evaluated how well he performed during the Cumberland Gap operation and evacuation.

In the end, General Morgan proved to be an able commander who made sound military decisions. Doctor B. F. Stevenson, a physician assigned to the 22nd Kentucky Infantry Regiment, was correct in predicting that some day General Morgan's decision to abandon Cumberland Gap would be vindicated.

Chapter 1
Political Situation

Cumberland Gap is a natural pass located at Middlesboro, Kentucky, that provides natural access to Kentucky, Tennessee, and Virginia through the Cumberland Plateau. Native Americans first used the pass to travel north to the Great Lakes, south to the Cherokee and Catawba empires, or northeast to the Iroquois Confederacy of Five Nations.[1] In 1673 Abraham Wood, a seventeenth century colonist, sent James Needham and Gabriel Arthur to explore the western wilderness. Needham died from a gunshot wound while on the expedition, but Arthur survived and was the first white man in recorded history to see Cumberland Gap.[2] However, he failed to realize the significance of his discovery. Seventy-six years later the Loyal Land Company employed Dr. Thomas Walker to locate 800,000 acres in western Virginia suitable for settlement. During his search on April 13, 1750, he stumbled upon Cumberland Gap. He recorded in his journal the following description of Cumberland Gap:

We went four miles to large Creek, which we called Cedar Creek, being a branch of Bear-Grass, and from thence Six miles to Cave Gap, the land being levil. On the North side of the Gap is a large Spring, which falls very fast, and just above the Spring is a small Entrance to a large Cave, which the Spring runs through, and there is a constant Stream of Cool air issuing out. The Spring is sufficient to turn a Mill. . . On the South side is a plain Indian Road. On top of the Ridge are Laurel Trees mark with crosses, others Blazed and several Figures on them . . . . The Mountain on the North Side of the Gap is very Steep and rocky, but on the South side it is not So. We called it Steep Ridge. At the foot of the hill on the North West Side we came to a Branch, that made a great deal of flat Land. We kept down it 2 miles, Several other Branches Coming in to make it a large Creek, and we called it Flat Creek. We camped on the Bank where we found very good Coal . . . .[3]

Dr. Walker named the gap Cumberland in honor of the Duke of Cumberland, an English war hero.[4]

Photograph taken by Lewis D. Nicholls at Cumberland Gap, Kentucky.

The Cumberland Plateau extends southwestward for 450 miles from southern West Virginia to northern Alabama, and extends 40 to 50 miles in width. The Gap is located where Kentucky, Tennessee, and Virginia intersect.[5] Civil War military planners on both sides considered Cumberland Gap a very strategic location dividing Confederate East Tennessee from neutral Kentucky. Consequently, Confederate and Union forces fought constantly for its control from 1861 to 1863.

During the Civil War, Kentucky was a neutral state. On May 16, 1861, the Kentucky Legislature declared its neutrality in a vote of 69-29. The Legislature resolved that:

This state and the citizens thereof shall take no part in the Civil War now being waged, except as mediators and friends to the belligerent parties; and that Kentucky should, during the contest, occupy a position of strict neutrality.[6]

The Kentucky Senate adopted its version of the statement. On May 20, 1861, Kentucky Governor Beriah Magoffin declared Kentucky's neutrality after passing both the House and Senate.

Now that Kentucky had declared its neutrality, Abraham Lincoln was extremely concerned that any false political move would drive Kentucky into the Confederate camp. Lincoln had good reason to be concerned since Kentucky had the third largest white population among the Confederate states. In fact, Kentucky, Missouri, and Maryland were all three slave states that had not yet joined the Confederacy. Their combined impact on the Confederacy's ability to wage war, "would have added 45 percent to the white population and military manpower of the Confederacy, 80 percent to its manufacturing capacity, and nearly 40 percent to its supply of horses and mules."[7] Kentucky ranked ninth in the nation in population, seventh in the value of farms, and fifth in the value of livestock.[8] Soon after the Civil War began, President Lincoln stated, "I think to lose Kentucky is nearly the same as to lose the whole game. Kentucky gone, we can not hold Missouri, nor, as I think, Maryland. These all against us, and the job on our hands is too large for us. We would as well consent to separation at once, including the surrender of this capitol."[9]

On June 20, 1861, Kentucky held its Federal congressional election. The pro-Union faction won nine of ten seats. On August 5, 1861, Kentucky held its state election. The pro-Union faction won 76 seats in the legislature while the pro-Confederate faction won 24 seats.

The pro-Union faction won 27 seats in the senate while the pro-Confederate faction won 11 seats. Clearly, a majority of Kentuckians wanted to remain in the Union. [10]

Some Kentuckians used the polls to rally support for their cause, while other Kentuckians prepared for war. Shortly after the August 5, 1861 election, President Lincoln opened a Federal recruiting station at the newly established Camp Dick Robinson in Garrard County approximately 35 miles south of Lexington, Kentucky. [11] Federal Senator John J. Crittenden complained to President Lincoln that Camp Dick Robinson was a violation of Kentucky's neutrality and should be disbanded. President Lincoln replied, "Taking all the means within my reach to form a judgment, I do not believe it is the popular wish of Kentucky that this force shall be removed beyond her limits; and, with this impression, I must respectfully decline to so remove it." [12]

Kentucky Governor Beriah Magoffin attempted to steer Kentucky on a neutral course despite his support for slavery. He even supported the right of a state to secede from the Union; however, he failed to support immediate secession. Governor Magoffin called for a conference of all slave and pro-Union states. [13] At this conference, the parties could present their different positions and work out mutually agreed rights with respect to slavery. These seemingly incompatible viewpoints made President Lincoln extremely nervous and caused most Union observers to believe that Kentucky could be steered into the Confederacy.

During this time, Inspector General Simon B. Buckner commanded the predominately pro-Confederate state military force known as the State Guards. They drilled and looked for weapons in preparation for war. To offset the pro-Confederate State Guards, Union sympathizers established local Home Guard military units. These Home Guard units began to secretly arm with weapons provided by the Union. [14]

By the end of August 1861, most Confederate supporters advocated that Kentucky remain neutral. However, most Kentuckians believed that if the Bluegrass State took a side, it should side with the Union. [15] The summer of 1861 was a particularly tense time for Kentucky as its official neutrality policy hung by a precarious thread.

Both Union and Confederate commanders recognized that the Mississippi River, on the western border of Kentucky, was of tremendous strategic importance. The Union could isolate the Confederate States from the western states by controlling the Mississippi River. Consequently, Confederate troops would be unable to use the Mississippi River as a supply line for the valuable supplies necessary to sustain a war. Thus, small river towns such as Columbus, Kentucky, took on renewed importance. Columbus was important not only because of its location on the Mississippi River, but because the Mobile & Ohio Railroad ran through it. This railroad ran deep into the South terminating at Mobile, Alabama. Whoever held Columbus could control the Mississippi River and the Mobile & Ohio Railroad.

On September 4, 1861, Confederate General Leonidas Polk, an Episcopal bishop turned general, ordered General Gideon Pillow to seize Columbus, Kentucky. General Pillow seized Columbus carrying out General Polk's order. In response, Union General Ulysses S. Grant seized Paducah, Kentucky, on the Ohio River. General Polk's order to seize Columbus infuriated Kentuckians by violating Kentucky's neutrality. Governor Magoffin chided both sides for "equally palpable and open violations of the neutral rights of Kentucky." [16]

A pro-Confederate legislator introduced a resolution in the Kentucky General Assembly to order both sides to withdraw from Kentucky soil, but the Legislature defeated the resolution, much to pro-Confederate Governor Magoffin's dismay. Consequently, Governor Magoffin vetoed the resolution. In response, the Legislature overrode the veto by a vote of 68-26 in the House and 25-9 in the

Senate. [16] As a result, General Polk's seizing of Columbus, Kentucky, proved to be an unwise political move because it succeeded in providing the spark that drove Kentucky inevitably into the Union camp.

With Kentucky apparently in the grip of the Union, Confederate war planners realized that Cumberland Gap was a strategic pass for several reasons. First, it provided a conduit through which pro-Union East Tennesseeans could move into Kentucky and fill the ranks of the Union Army. Second, the Union Army could launch a thrust through the Gap and seize Knoxville and cripple the combined railroads of the East Tennessee & Georgia and East Tennessee & Virginia. This would severely limit the Confederate's ability to shuffle troops and supplies between the eastern and western regions of the Confederacy. Third, the Confederacy could launch an invasion into Kentucky and recruit Kentuckians into the Confederate army. Therefore, both sides thought it was imperative to control Cumberland Gap.

Today, most people believe that Tennessee was a Confederate state. But, that is only half of the picture. On May 24, 1861, the Tennessee governor declared Tennessee a member of the Confederacy. However, a large portion of east Tennesseeans supported the Union cause and refused to recognize the Tennessee governor's declaration. They called for secession of East Tennessee from the rest of the state.[17] When East Tennesseeans began to migrate into southeastern Kentucky to join the Union cause, Lincoln sent Navy Lieutenant William Nelson into eastern Kentucky to established Camp Dick Robinson in Garrard County, Kentucky, for the purpose of receiving these men into the Union army. Lincoln chose Nelson because he was a popular native Kentuckian.

Lincoln also chose Naval officer Samuel P. Carter to muster into service three infantry regiments to conduct offensive and defensive operations in southeastern Kentucky and northeastern Tennessee. [18] Lincoln chose Carter because he was a popular northeastern Tenneseean who supported the Union cause. Carter established a recruiting center to receive the East Tennesseans two miles east of Barbourville, Kentucky.[19] Lincoln granted both Carter and Nelson army commissions as they began their recruiting and training duties.

With these developments, Confederate war planners worried that Cumberland Gap could be used as a staging area and jumping off point for a Union thrust into East Tennessee. East Tennessee was extremely important to the Confederacy because it was, ". . . one of the largest wheat-producing areas in the south, as well as a region blessed with abundant resources of saltpeter, lead, and copper. The Confederacy's ability to feed its soldiers and produce gunpowder, bullets, percussion caps, and bronze artillery would be damaged if East Tennessee were in Union hands." [20]

The East Tennessee & Georgia Railroad ran from Chattanooga to Knoxville. From Knoxville, the East Tennessee & Virginia Railroad extended to Bristol and then on to Richmond, Virginia. If the Union could penetrate into Tennessee far enough and sever this railroad, then Confederate supplies and men would have to be moved through Atlanta, Georgia, to connect with Richmond, Virginia. This long and circuitous path would severely reduce response time for the Confederacy to repel Union incursions into the eastern theater of operations.[21] Likewise, Confederate war planners were very concerned that a well-timed Union thrust through Cumberland Gap could sever the East Tennessee & Georgia Railroad since the line ran only 40-50 miles from the Gap. [22]

Many Southerners believed that should the Confederacy invade the Bluegrass Commonwealth, many Kentuckians would flock to the Southern cause and fill the ranks of the Confederate Army. When Confederate General Kirby Smith invaded Kentucky in July 1862, he thought he could hold all of Kentucky with 25,000 to 30,000 men. [23] Many Kentuckians disliked high-handed Federal authorities who violated their civil rights; however, this failed to translate into volunteers for the Confederate Army. [24] Actually, this was only the

fantasy thinking of pro-Confederate political supporters. Nevertheless, they convinced enough Southerners to influence military plan-
ning.

During July 1861, the Confederate War Department sent Brigadier General Felix Kirk Zollicoffer to East Tennessee to settle down
the pro-Union uprising among the civilian population. General
Zollicoffer seized Cumberland Gap with only three infantry regiments
and three pieces of artillery. [25] By the end of September 1861,
Zollicoffer had approximately 2,700 men assembled in the
Cumberland Gap area. [26] Zollicoffer penetrated deeper into Kentucky, eventually bringing his troop strength to approximately 4000
men. Confederate President Jefferson Davis then appointed George
B. Crittenden to assume command of the Confederate force being led
by Zollicoffer. [27] This command change added confusion to an already complicated operation with an ill-equipped army in a wilderness during the beginning of winter, with little or no supplies and
horrible roads. A Union force under the command of Brigadier General George H. Thomas stopped the Confederate incursion at the Battle
of Mill Springs on January 19, 1862 near present day Jamestown, Kentucky.   Union sharpshooters killed General Zollicoffer as he rode
toward a Union position mistaking it for his own line during the "fog
of war." [28] Crittenden reported 125 killed, 309 wounded, and 95 missing. Thomas reported 40 killed, 207 wounded, and 15 missing. [29]
Crittenden then retreated to Gainesboro, Tennessee, to regroup and
refit. [30]

Crittenden probably left some elements of his force at
Cumberland Gap to prevent any Union incursion into East Tennessee during the winter. By March 1, 1862, the Confederate force grew
to approximately 5,000 troops at the Gap.[31] Confederate leadership
concerned itself with possible gaps that the Union could utilize to
penetrate into East Tennessee. These included, "Big Chitwood Gap,
10 miles north of Huntsville, good road, easily crossed by an army;

Elk Fork Gap, horse road and not used by wagons; Old Wheeler's 3 ½ miles south of Jacksborough, wagon road blocked up by General Zollicoffer, but it is said that horsemen abound on the hillside; and Big Creek Gap, good road, and the one which it is conjectured the Yankees will most probably take." [32] This conjecture proved to be prophetic because that was in fact the route the 7th Division of the Union Army under the command of Brigadier George W. Morgan used to retake Cumberland Gap in June 1862.

Chapter 2
Military Situation

Major General Don Carlos Buell commanded the Department of the Ohio that was comprised of seven divisions. Brig. Gen. George W. Morgan commanded one of these divisions. General Buell located his headquarters at Louisville, Kentucky. General Henry Wager Halleck, known as "Old Brains" because of his intelligence, commanded the Department of the Missouri. The Ohio and Missouri departments were divided by the Cumberland River.[1] Another department was the Department of Kansas. This fragmented structure made command and control very awkward in the Western theater and encouraged competition among the generals instead of cooperation.[2]

Ulysses S. Grant and Andrew H. Foote were under the command of General Halleck. In February 1862 they captured Fort Donelson on the Cumberland River and Fort Henry on the Tennessee River. The capture of Fort Donelson provided an avenue of transportation for the Union army all the way to the Capitol of Tennessee at Nashville. The Confederates abandoned Nashville and the Federals captured it one week later. This was a severe blow to the Southern cause because Nashville manufactured, ". . . all manner of war supplies, from heavy ordnance to shoes, flour, and bacon." [3] In addition to the loss of this manufacturing capability, Nashville was also an important railroad junction for the Nashville & Decatur, Nashville & Chattanooga, and Louisville & Nashville railroads.

The Union's capture of Fort Henry on the Tennessee River and Fort Donelson on the Cumberland River provided a water route for the flow of supplies and troops into the heart of Dixie. In fact, the fall of these two forts initiated the ultimate collapse of the Confederacy in the West. Historians can make a credible argument that the collapse of these two forts punched a small hole in the artery of the Confederacy that caused it to slowly bleed to death in five years ultimately at Appomattox, Virginia. [4]

On March 11, 1862 the War Department in Washington consolidated the Department of the Missouri, Department of Kansas and the western part of the Department of the Ohio into the Department of the Mississippi. They appointed General Halleck as commander of the Department of the Mississippi giving him authority over General Buell. [5] Now, command decisions would be unified and hopefully facilitate a more efficient use of men and material.

General Halleck divided his army of approximately 100,000 men into several task forces. He sent General William Tecumseh Sherman to Memphis and General John McClernand to Jackson, Tennessee. [6] He sent General Buell east to seize Chattanooga with a force of approximately 35,000 soldiers. Chattanooga was an important junction for several railroads. From Chattanooga The Western & Atlantic Railroad ran to Atlanta, Georgia; the East Tennessee & Georgia Railroad ran to Knoxville; the Nashville & Chattanooga Railroad ran to Nashville; and the Memphis & Charleston Railroad ran to Memphis. The Tennessee River ran through Chattanooga also making it available as a means of transportation by water for the Union cause. Clearly, Chattanooga made an excellent strategic objective. If Buell could capture it, the Confederate cause would be dealt a serious blow.

General Buell counted on the railroads to transport his men and supplies to Chattanooga. What he didn't count on were small bands of Confederate troops destroying bridges and tunnels along the railroad, making it more difficult to supply the Union army. The Confederates effectively destroyed the bridges and tunnels significantly impeding the Union's ability to supply her troops. General Buell left small detachments of Union troops to guard each bridge or tunnel as he moved forward to Chattanooga. He also had engineers construct new bridges and tunnels. For a while Buell tried to supplement the slow progress of the railroad supply line with wagons, but there was just an insufficient number of wagons to transport the amount of food, ammunition, and other supplies necessary to supply the huge Federal army. Finally, General Halleck sent a message to General Buell in which he said:

The President telegraphs that your progress is not satisfactory and that you should move more rapidly. The long time taken by you to reach Chattanooga will enable the enemy to anticipate you by concentrating a large force to meet you. I communicate his views, hoping that your movements hereafter may be so rapid as to remove all cause of complaint, whether well founded or not. [7]

On March 26, 1862 General Buell placed Brig. General George Washington Morgan in command of the 7th Division and ordered him to take Cumberland Gap.[8] General Morgan rode in a buggy from Lexington, Kentucky, to Cumberland Ford (present day Pineville, Ky.) to assume command of the 7th Division.[9] Along the way he encountered narrow roads winding through high mountains. It rained so heavily that horses had to

Brigadier-General **George W. Morgan** *Battles and Leaders of Civil War Vol. III.*

swim in many places. A small train of twelve or so wagons could only make three to four miles a day.[10]

ORGANIZATION OF UNION 7TH DIVISION

			DEPT OF MISS HALLECK				
			ARMY OF OHIO BUELL				
			7TH DIV G. MORGAN				
24TH BGD CARTER	**25TH BGD SPEARS**	**26TH BGD DECOURCY**	**27TH BGD BAIRD**	**ARTILLERY FOSTER**	**CAVALRY MUNDAY**	**ENGINEERS PATTERSON**	

49TH IND	3RD TENN	22ND KY	33RD IND	7TH MICH		Infantry Regiment
7TH KY	4TH TENN	16TH OHIO	14TH KY	9TH OHIO		Artillery Battery
1ST TENN	5TH TENN	42ND OHIO	19TH KY	1ST WI		Engineer Unit
2ND TENN	6TH TENN			SIEGE BATTERY		Cavalry Unit

General Morgan found one of his brigades, General Carter's, on the verge of scurvy. The northern side of Cumberland Gap was incapable of producing enough hay to feed the horses and mules. It became necessary to bring in hay from distances as far as ninety miles to feed the livestock. Morgan then ordered a bridge built over the Cumberland River and used it to bring in fresh meat for the troops who had not had any for three months.[11]

General Morgan also found that many regiments were armed with rifles of different calibers, making resupply a logistical night-mare. Ammunition was in very short supply. He corrected these problems, as best he could, then began military operations.[12]

The 7th Division was comprised of four brigades of infantry with three to four regiments each, an artillery unit made up of four batteries, a cavalry battalion, and a company of engineers. Most of the Division ranks were filled by Kentuckians and Tennesseeans. However, a few units from Indiana, Ohio, Michigan, and Wisconsin also filled the unit rosters.[13] Approximately 10,000 Union troops comprised the 7th Division.

Brig. Gen. Samuel P. Carter commanded the 24th Brigade. General Carter was the Navy Lieutenant sent by President Lincoln to Eastern Kentucky to recruit Tennesseeans loyal to the Union. The 24th Brigade was comprised of the 49th Indiana Regiment commanded by Lt. Col. James Keigwin; the 7th Kentucky Regiment commanded by Col. T.T. Garrard; the 1st Tennessee Regiment commanded by Col. Robert K. Byrd; and the 2nd Tennessee Regiment commanded by Col. James P.T. Carter.[14]

Brig. Gen. James G. Spears commanded the 25th Brigade, an all Tennessee unit comprised of the 3rd Tennessee commanded by Col. Leonidas C. Houk, the 4th Tennessee commanded by Col. Robert Johnson, the 5th Tennessee commanded by Col. James T. Shelly, and the 6th Tennessee commanded by Col. Joseph A. Cooper.[15]

Col. John F. DeCourcy commanded the 26th Brigade.[16] Col. DeCourcy, "an Irish soldier of fortune" commanded both Ohio and Kentucky troops in the 26th Regiment.[17] It was comprised of the 22nd Kentucky commanded by Col. Daniel W. Lindsey; the 16th Ohio commanded by Lt. Col. George W. Bailey; and the 42nd Ohio commanded by Col. Lionel A. Sheldon.[18]

Brig. Gen. Absalom Baird commanded the 27th Brigade. General Baird was later awarded the Medal of Honor on April 22, 1896, for his part in an assault on Confederate positions on September 1, 1863, at Jonesboro, Georgia.[19] General Baird's Brigade was comprised of the 33rd Indiana commanded by Col. John Coburn, the 14th Kentucky commanded by Col. John Cochran, and the 19th Kentucky command by Col. William J. Landrum.[20]

Also attached to General Morgan's 7th Division were four artillery units under the command of Capt. Jacob T. Foster. These artillery units included the 7th Michigan commanded by Capt. Charles H. Lamphere, the 9th Ohio commanded by Lt. Leonard P. Barrows; the 1st Wisconsin commanded by Lt. John D. Anderson, and a Siege Battery commanded by Lt. Daniel Webster. Lt. Col. Reuben Munday commanded the Kentucky Battalion of cavalry, and Capt. William F. Patterson commanded the Kentucky Engineers.[21]

Lieutenant-General
E. Kirby Smith
Battles and Leaders of Civil War Vol. III.

General Buell commanded the Army of the Ohio that included seven divisions of approximately 62,000 men.[22] The 7th Division was the only Buell division located on the northern side of the Cumberland Mountains. Thus, communication between Gen. Buell and Gen. Morgan was extremely difficult. Buell had little effective command and control over the 7th Division. To compound the problem, Buell was unable to supply Morgan from the southern side of the Cumberland Mountains since the Confederates occupied Cumberland Gap. This forced Morgan to rely entirely on supply from Lexington, Kentucky, along roads that were nothing more than mule paths. This separation between the 7th Division and the rest of the Army of the Ohio left the 7th Division in a very precarious situation.

On March 9, 1862, Maj. General Edmund Kirby Smith, C.S.A., Confederate States of America, assumed command of the Confederate forces in East Tennessee.[23] Kirby Smith was a Floridian who graduated from West Point in 1845. He fought in the Mexican War winning two brevets that are higher honorary ranks without pay. He taught mathematics at West Point after the war. In 1855 he transferred into the cavalry where he fought Indians in Texas and was wounded there in 1859.[24]

Upon assuming command, Kirby Smith found approximately

4,000 Confederate forces at Cumberland Gap who were disorganized and in disarray. Colonel James E. Rains, C.S.A. commanded the Confederate troops at the Gap.[25]

On March 20, 1862, Col. Samuel P. Carter of the 24th Brigade received word that the Second East Tennessee Regiment was about to be attacked by some of Kirby Smith's troops. Consequently, Col. Morgan ordered the 1st East Tennessee, 7th Kentucky, 16th Ohio, 49th Indiana, the 1st Battalion of Kentucky Cavalry, and a battery of the 9th Ohio Artillery, under the command of Gen. Samuel P. Carter, ready to move. He ordered four days' rations be dispersed to the troops. They left from Camp Cumberland Ford and approached the Gap. The next day the two armies engaged in an artillery duel. Carter remained just in front of the Gap and used the encounter to gather intelligence on the Confederate forces. During this two-day contact with the Confederate forces, it snowed, stormed and sleeted. Despite bivouacking under these conditions, they remained long enough for Col. Carter to form the opinion that, ". . . the place [Cumberland Gap] is very strong if attacked from the north side, and can only be carried by a large force with a heavy loss of life, but it can be readily reduced by having a good force attack simultaneously on the south side, or, better still, by an investment, which would soon starve them out."[26] Interestingly, General Smith and Col. Rains estimated the Union forces at between 4,000 and 6,000 when in fact the Union had only 2,900.[27]

After solving some of his logistical problems, Morgan personally conducted a reconnaissance of the Confederate troop locations on April 11, 1862. On April 28, 1862, Morgan sent Carter and DeCourcy to conduct further reconnaissance of the Gap.[28] Their intelligence revealed that the Confederates were shifting troops back and forth along the Cumberland Mountain Range. This reconnaissance continued until June 1862 when General Morgan decided that the time was right to attempt to seize Cumberland Gap.

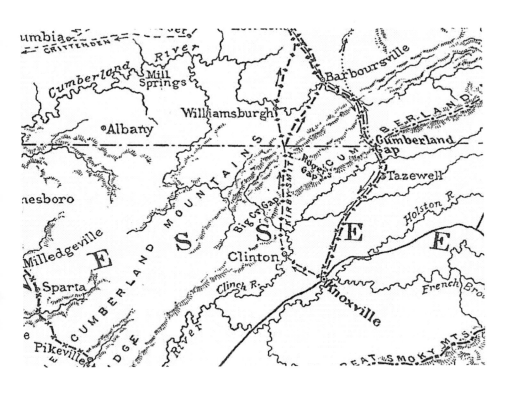

Map is taken from Battles and Leaders, Volume III

Chapter 3
Union Takes Cumberland Gap

General Morgan decided that a frontal assault on Cumberland Gap would be too costly. Consequently, he devised a plan where his troops would move to the west during darkness and cross the Cumberland Mountains at Rogers Gap and Big Creek Gap. Rogers Gap was 20 miles west of Cumberland Gap, and Big Creek was 15 miles west of Rogers Gap. Morgan's plan called for DeCourcy's and Baird's Brigades to cross over Roger's Gap, and Spears' and Carter's Brigades to cross over Big Creek Gap. Spears and Carter would then rendezvous with DeCourcy's and Baird's Brigades on the southern base of Roger's Gap in the Powell Valley in northeastern Tennessee. Morgan's plan also called for the artillery to cross the gaps — a military feat, up to this time, considered to be impossible. Once reunited, the four brigades would travel along the Powell Valley and attack Cumberland Gap from the south side.

On May 22, 1862, Morgan sent De Courcy's Brigade forward to construct a small fort about four miles south of Pineville. He manned this bogus fort with troops that were unfit for duty due to medical reasons. This was designed to confuse the Confederates as to his real intention which was to slide his Division west and cross

Roger's and Big Creek Gaps. He even placed explosive charges on the mountain sides near Pineville to explode if the Confederates somehow started to get in his rear thereby protecting his supply line from Lexington. Fortunately, it never became necessary to detonate these charges.

Morgan put the plan into action by sending General Spears with three regiments to clear out a road blocked with trees and rocks on the way to Big Creek Gap. The Confederates responded by stationing in front of Big Creek Gap, "two brigades of infantry, two regiments of cavalry, and two batteries of artillery."[1] Confederate General Kirby Smith sent a large detachment of infantry across Woodson's Gap to cut off Spears. General Morgan received a report, just in time, from a lady sympathetic to the Union cause by the name of Mrs. Edwards, informing him of the Confederate advance on Spears. Consequently, Morgan sent a courier who reached Spears in time ordering him to pull back to Barbourville to escape General Smith's trap.

On June 6, 1862, General Morgan sent the advance guard forward consisting of Munday's cavalry and the 3rd Tennessee Infantry. Next in the order of march were the large cannons and artillery pieces, followed by De Courcy's brigade, Baird's brigade, and then Carter's brigade. A battery of artillery brought up the rear. They began from Cumberland Ford and marched toward Cumberland Gap on the Old State Road also known as the Cumberland Gap Road. They marched to the Moss house about two miles from Cumberland Ford which was located at the junction of State Road and a pathway turning to the right leading to Lambdin's house, which was located four miles west of the junction. [2] Morgan received word that Kirby Smith had withdrawn into the Powell Valley on the south side of the Cumberland Mountains.

During this advance, Morgan had work parties in front of the column widening the road, which was nothing more than a horse path, so heavy artillery could pass over it. Morgan also had other work parties at the end of the Union column blocking the road so that a Confederate patrol could not surprise them. Morgan reported that "old men, women, and children flocked to the roadside, and everywhere we were welcomed with smiles and tears of joy."[3]

Captain J. T. Foster commanded the artillery for the 7th Division as the Chief of Artillery. They took up the line of march immediately behind Munday's cavalry. [4] They had to use block and tackle and at one point had 200 men pulling drag ropes up and down the mountainous pathways.[5] They encountered steep cliffs, ". . . varying in height from one hundred to five hundred feet." [6] Roads turned at angles exceeding 90 degrees and in many instances the road was too narrow to turn around a team of horses.[7] Many of the men in the artillery train had traveled to California and declared that these Cumberland Mountains were much more difficult to climb than the passes they crossed over the Rocky Mountains.[8] By June 12, 1862, the artillery train entered the south side of Rogers Gap ready to join the rest of the Division.

Col. De Courcy began the march of his 26th Brigade on June 7, 1862. They traveled only eight miles the first day because of the bad roads and steep terrain.[9] On June 8, 1862, the 26th Brigade traveled thirteen miles. Col. De Courcy detailed 300 men to help haul the wagons over the hills.[10] The next day, the column made the last eight miles, but it was held up for eight hours as the last two miles required construction of a new road.[11] On June 10, 1862, they reached the foot of the north side of Rogers Gap. When the Confederates saw such a large force coming at them, they abandoned Rogers Gap but blocked the road everywhere possible to cause the Union trouble negotiating the steep terrain. By the evening of June 11, 1862, the 26th Brigade bivouacked in the Powell Valley on the south side of Rogers Gap.[12]

On Sunday, June 9, 1862, Brigadier General A. Baird began the march with the 27th Brigade. It took them three days to reach the foot of Rogers Gap after a march of thirty-two miles. They rested on Wednesday, June 10, 1862, and then started the trip over Rogers Gap. Many of his units reached Powell Valley by the next day.

Brigadier General S. P. Carter, commanding the 24th Brigade, began the trek toward Big Creek Gap on June 8, 1862. By June 12 they reached Lambdin's house where they received an order from a courier to proceed to Williamsburg, Kentucky. [13] They took the right fork on the road at Lambdin's house and headed toward Williamsburg. The next day they received another dispatch to proceed to the south side of Big Creek Gap in the Powell Valley. The 24th Brigade reached Big Creek Gap on June 16 just in time to support Brigadier General James G. Spears' 25th Brigade who had come from Barbourville.

On June 11, 1862, Brigadier General James G. Spears, commanding the 25th Brigade, entered Big Creek Gap. He immediately encountered an ambush, but he eventually dislodged the Confederates. The Confederates suffered two killed and several wounded.[14] The 25th Brigade encountered several skirmishes at Big Creek Gap, but eventually Spears' troops repulsed the enemy and descended into the Powell Valley.[15]

General Morgan did not operate in a vacuum independent of the other Union troops south of the Cumberland Mountains. He knew that military units operated through teamwork. Thus, on June 8, 1862, he sent a message to General Buell asking what General James S. Negley was doing.[16] General Negley led a force of 9,000 Union troops operating close to Chattanooga.[17] Morgan hoped that Negley could put pressure on Chattanooga and draw Confederate General Kirby Smith away from Cumberland Gap. On June 12, 1862, General Morgan received two messages from General Buell. The first message was dated June 9, 1862 and stated:

General Morgan, Cumberland Ford:

General Negley is fully employed in Middle Tennessee, and can give you no direct assistance. He is, however, opposite Chattanooga, but his stay there cannot be depended upon. The force now in Tennessee is so small that no offensive operations against East Tennessee can be attempted, and you must therefore depend mainly on your own resources.

D. C. Buell,

Major-General, Commanding

The second message was dated June 10, 1862 and stated:

Headquarters, June 10, 1862

Considering your force and that opposed to you, it will probably not be safe for you to undertake any extended offensive operations. Other operations will soon have an influence upon your designs, and it is therefore better for you to run no risk at present.

James B. Fry,

Colonel and Chief of Staff[18]

General Morgan now had a clear message that he could not depend on General Negley for any assistance. He had a clear order not to conduct any offensive operations that would be risky. Clearly, attacking Cumberland Gap from the rear was risky business because Kirby Smith occupied Knoxville and threatened to cut off Morgan, capturing his entire force. Then, there would be nothing to stop Kirby Smith from invading Kentucky. If Kirby Smith invaded Kentucky, it could have catastrophic results if the political rumors were true that Kentuckians were ready to rise up and join the ranks of the Confederacy.

By the time General Morgan received the message from Colonel Fry, dated June 10, 1862, he already had troops on top of Big Creek Gap and Rogers Gap. In fact by June 12, 1862, De Courcy's and Baird's brigades were on the south side of Rogers Gap in the Powell Valley. Despite their success in reaching the Powell Valley, General Morgan ordered them to march back over the mountains once again into Kentucky. Many of these troops were Tennesseeans, and they were extremely disappointed that they would be unable to enter Tennessee and liberate their loved ones in pro-Union East Tennessee.

On June 13, 1862, General Morgan received another message from General Buell that stated:

> *Headquarters, June 11, 1862*
> *General Morgan, Cumberland For:*
> *General Negley has been withdrawn from before Chattanooga, but General Mitchell is instructed as far as possible to keep his troops in a position to threaten that point. As you were previously advised, you will have to depend mainly upon your own ability to beat the force opposed to you.*
> *D. C. Buell,*
> *Major — General, Commanding* [19]

General Morgan's interpretation of this message would later prove to be controversial. After General Morgan withdrew from Cumberland Gap, this message gave politicians in Washington, D. C. a reason to blame him for failing to follow orders. General Morgan was at Lambdin's house when he received it, and he showed the message to Col. De Courcy. They discussed it and finally General Morgan came to the conclusion that the last phrase in the message, ". . . you will have to depend mainly upon your own ability to beat the force opposed to you" as authority at his discretion to proceed with the attack on Cumberland Gap.[20] Morgan invoked his legal training to interpret the ambiguous message. Words are the means of a lawyer's craft, and this phrase, seemingly inconsistent with the other messages he received, provided Morgan with sufficient political cover

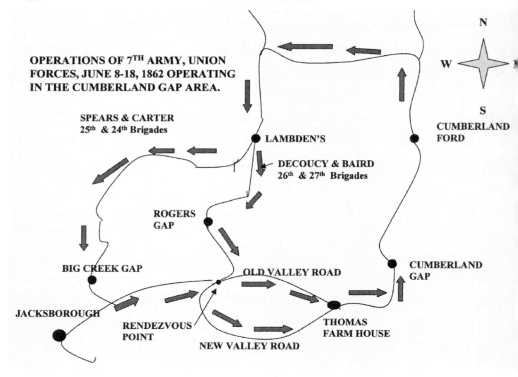

OPERATIONS OF 7TH ARMY, UNION FORCES, JUNE 8-18, 1862 OPERATING IN THE CUMBERLAND GAP AREA.

SPEARS & CARTER
25th & 24th Brigades

LAMBDEN'S

DECOUCY & BAIRD
26th & 27th Brigades

ROGERS GAP

BIG CREEK GAP

OLD VALLEY ROAD

CUMBERLAND FORD

CUMBERLAND GAP

JACKSBOROUGH

RENDEZVOUS POINT

THOMAS FARM HOUSE

NEW VALLEY ROAD

N

W

S

to justify resuming the attack on Cumberland Gap. He reasoned that he could rely on his, "own ability to beat the force opposed", at Cumberland Gap. On the same day, Morgan received a message from Colonel De Courcy that the Confederates were abandoning Cumberland Gap. Morgan concluded that General Buell would approve of carrying forward with the attack on Cumberland Gap, particularly if he could seize it, if actually abandoned by the Confederates. Clearly, General Morgan was a leader who was not afraid to make tough decisions and take the initiative. These were characteristics sorely lacking in Union commanders at this time. Thus, for the "third time in forty-eight hours," Morgan ordered his troops back across Rogers Gap.[21] Despite extreme fatigue, his troops responded with a renewed determination to seize Cumberland Gap from the Confederates. By June 14, 1862, De Courcy's brigade arrived on the south side of Rogers Gap.[22] Baird's brigade rendezvoused with De Courcy's brigade on June 15, 1862. As Baird's brigade marched down the mountain, the 33rd Indiana Regimental band played "Dixie" to emphasize the fact that they had arrived in Confederate territory.[23] Spears' and Carter's brigades arrived the next day. Morgan was ready to march toward the Gap, but Spears' and Carter's troops were extremely fatigued after the seventy-five mile long march from Big Creek Gap. Consequently, Morgan decided to rest his troops one day before beginning the march to the Gap because of the fatigued state of Spears' and Carter's brigades.[24]

Morgan devised a plan for the march to Cumberland Gap in which Spears' brigade would start at 1:00 a.m. on June 18, 1862, and march along the Old Valley Road. De Courcy's brigade would begin marching at 1:30 a.m. and follow Spears' brigade on the Old Valley Road. Baird's brigade would bring up the rear on the same road and begin his march at 2:00 a.m. Carter's brigade would screen for the other three brigades by marching along the New Valley Road on the southern side and parallel to the Old Valley Road.[25] Morgan expected a fight at Thomas's farm, but the Confederate evacuation of the Gap was completed by 10 a.m.

When the Union troops arrived at Cumberland Gap, Union soldier G. W. Reeder, in a letter to his aunt and uncle, described that the Confederates left behind, "350 tents and the provisions. It was a sight, and cooking utensils of all sorts and clothing of all sorts and cots to sleep on and bed clothes, axes and spades and picks and a little of everything—they left a big cannon though they spiked it, and threw four of them over a clift, [cliff]—we got one of the 64-pounders and unspiked it."[26]

General Morgan reported, "The same afternoon the national colors were unfurled, and a national salute was fired from the summit of the gap by De Courcy's brigade, and by a general order each brigade was authorized to unfurl its colors, amid the roar of cannon, upon the pinnacle of the mountain, for the honor belongs equally to all." Morgan sent Carter's brigade as far as Tazewell in pursuit of the retreating Confederates, but they safely hid in the Clinch Mountains.[27] Not one single Union life had been lost in taking Cumberland Gap. Next, Morgan planned to march against Knoxville and requested "two additional brigades of infantry, a battery, and two regiments of cavalry." [28] Unfortunately, General Buell denied his request. Buell was content to have Morgan sit on top of Cumberland Gap preventing Kirby Smith from coming through it into Kentucky, or so he thought.

Chapter 4
Union Occupation Of Cumberland Gap — Summer 1862

On June 18, 1862, the 7th Division seized Cumberland Gap from the Confederates. Any good military commander would expect a counterattack against a recently seized position, and General Morgan was no exception. He quickly ordered his men to strengthen the fortifications already constructed by the Confederate Army. He ordered his men to construct, "nine south-facing batteries to repel an invasion." [1] These fortifications added to the already existing, "seven forts on the north facing slope" constructed by the Confederates. Of course, Morgan was not guarding against a northern attack. The Confederates also cleared the "mountains of all trees within one mile of each fort." [2] Clearing the trees created unimpeded fields of fire insuring that Morgan's troops could not be sneaked up on, and it created effective killing zones. Morgan once again demonstrated his sound understanding of military principles, complying with the principle of security.

The Confederates took their artillery with them when they abandoned the Gap, but they left seven large cannons including a special Parrott artillery piece that was too heavy and large to move. England made three of these special Parrott guns and delivered them to the South before the outbreak of hostilities. These artillery pieces loaded from the breech, back of the gun, and were rifled. Rifling was a process where grooves were cut inside the barrel to give the shell a spin as it was fired out of the muzzle. This stabilized the shell in flight, giving it greater accuracy. Robert Parker Parrott, an American, invented the gun. This artillery piece could fire loaded shells or heavy shot. [3] Loaded shells had explosive charges in them that exploded by time or on impact. Heavy shot most likely referred to solid round balls particularly useful against personnel at long ranges.

To insure that the Parrott artillery piece was of no use to the invading Union army, the Confederates "spiked" it, and pushed it off the edge of the cliff. "Spiked" means they drove a piece of metal, sometimes a rattail file, into the vent located atop the breech of the piece, causing it to be incapable of being fired. [4] However, Morgan's troops found the Parrott piece at the bottom of the cliff and repaired it. They then drug it to the top of the cliff and pointed it in a southerly direction.

Establishing defensive positions was easy compared to trying to keep this large army supplied. Keeping the 7th Division in food and supplies rapidly became a logistical nightmare. Morgan placed over 400 wagons in small trains on the roads from his supply base in central Kentucky.[5] However, even 400 wagons hauling food and supplies proved to be insufficient for the logistical needs of the 7th Division. Thus, it became necessary for the troops to look for food from additional sources.

Morgan sent out seven foraging expeditions while they occupied Cumberland Gap looking for the necessary supplies. [6] On one such occasion on August 2, 1862, Morgan sent De Courcy on a foraging expedition near Tazwell, Tennessee. Morgan's men found 200 wagonloads of forage that safely arrived back at Cumberland Gap on August 5, 1862. On August 6, 1862, De Courcy was returning to the Gap when Confederate soldiers attacked his expedition. Two regiments of Confederate soldiers trapped two companies of the 16th Ohio by surrounding them, but the 16th Ohio fought their way out of the trap.

Confederate re-enactors repulsing a Union foraging expedition looking for food near Cumberland Gap. Photograph taken by Lewis D. Nicholls.

During the engagement, Morgan described the heroic efforts of one Union soldier.

"A soldier of the Twenty-second Kentucky was shot through the neck and fell. His gun dropped from his hands; his foe contrived to advance upon him, when the wounded hero grasped his gun, rose to his feet and shot the rebel soldier dead when within five paces of him, when he again fell weltering in his blood." [7]

Inadequate food for the 7th Division created an ominous warning that the Union soldiers could not remain long at Cumberland Gap. The inadequate road system in eastern Kentucky created an impaired ability to resupply the 7th Division. In fact, the only road that could support the kind of traffic necessary to resupply the 7th Division was the Mount Sterling-Pound Gap Road. Unfortunately, this road did not come close enough to Cumberland Ford to be of much help to the Union army at Cumberland Gap. "It began at Mount Sterling and extended through Hazel Green, Licking Station, Prestonsburg, Laynesville and Pikeville to the Virginia State Line at Pound Gap." [8] Morgan's troops would have to use "roads" that were nothing more than horse paths to get from Hazel Green to Cumberland Ford. However, the roads from Hazel Green to Cumberland Ford were so bad that during the months of April and May, the rainy season, "a train of ten wagons could only advance 3 or 4 miles per day." [9] During the Civil War this road was the main thoroughfare for the military moving between Central and Eastern Kentucky. [10]

Inadequate roads were not the only problem the 7th Division encountered. The Division was composed of men who had the same personal needs we have today. They needed food, housing, and hygienic personal products. During the Civil War, "more men died of looseness of the bowels than fell on the field of combat." [11]   In the Union army, four men died from disease for every one that was killed in combat.[12] Peak sickness among Union and Confederate troops occurred during the months of July and August.[13]   In fact, there were four causes of death during the war in addition to the losses caused by actual combat.

First, the Union army took anyone who wanted to enlist at the beginning of the war. Thus, older and sickly men were more prone to disease. Since there existed a greater percentage of weaklings in the army, a greater number of them fell to the diseases that ravaged it.

Second, ignorance of disease contributed greatly to the problem. Flies and other insects prevalent at Cumberland Gap transmitted diseases. All they needed was an area of filth. Civil war soldiers called latrines "sinks", and they were present in every army that bivouacked.[14] There exists no record of where the latrines were located for the Union army at Cumberland Gap, but they must have been close to the living quarters because they caused a significant disease problem. Often soldiers failed to cover the excrement with dirt creating the right conditions for the insects to transmit diseases.

Third, army regulations required that the men wash their hands, faces, and take "baths once or twice a week."[15] However, most men failed to follow this regulation. In addition, many officers failed to enforce it.

Fourth, garbage disposal was a real problem. "Camp streets and spaces between the tents littered with refuse, food and other rubbish, sometimes in an offensive state of decomposition; slops deposited in pits within the camp limits or thrown out broadcast; heaps of manure and offal close to the camp."[16] Contemporary sketches of Cumberland Gap reveal that during the Union occupation during the summer of 1862, there existed a few wooden houses and structures, but most of the enlisted men lived in tents. It is highly likely that the men at Cumberland Gap lived under similar conditions as described above. All of these factors contributed to the filthy conditions that formed an excellent breeding ground that caused sickness among the troops.

Contributing to the misery, inadequate clothing, exposure to the elements, and poor nutrition compounded the military problems thrust upon the 7th Division.[17] In fact, during the month of April, Morgan stated that my "troops were half-famished and were suffering from scurvy. Of the 900 men of the 49th Indiana regiment, only 200 were fit for duty."[18] These conditions created the expected results of disease. On June 28, 1862, one soldier with the 2nd Tennessee, Paul Grogger, complained of illness. In his diary he states, "I began to take sick with fever and headache which our doctor announced to be typhoid fever. I had indeed a very severe spell of it as the fever fell all into my head, which almost proved to be fatal. All of my comrades as well as myself began to get hopeless for my life, which I no doubt would a fell victim of, had not your surgeon used all the ingenuity of his practice and exertion to raise me."[19] Morgan and his brigade commanders made no mention of illness and sickness among the troops except to praise, "Dr. B. Cloak, acting medical director, and the corps of surgeons under him" after they evacuated the Gap.[20]

Sickness and illness among the troops had a significant detrimental effect on the fighting capability of the 7th Division. During the Civil War, sickness due to disease and unsanitary conditions often significantly affected military readiness. Morgan reported that just prior to leaving Cumberland Gap on September 17, 1862, he had just over 10,000 men.[21] On September 10, 1862 Lieut. Charles S. Medary of the Third U. S. Artillery carried a message to Maj. Gen. H. G. Wright at Cincinnati, Ohio, giving him the status of the 7th Division. Medary later stated in a statement to the Buell Commission, "There was an effective force of between 7,000 and 8,000 men at the Gap."[22] Assuming 10,000 men at the Gap and 7,000 to 8,000 were effective, then 2,000 to 3,000 must have been ineffective. A reasonable supposition would be that these men were ill.

We know from the Memoirs of Paul Grogger that typhoid fever existed in the camp. A disease such as typhoid spreads through contaminated water and general unsanitary conditions. It requires no stretch of the imagination to conclude that other men had typhoid as well. A reporter with the *Cincinnati Daily Gazette* newspaper traveled with the 7th Division during the evacuation. In the October 6, 1862, edition of the newspaper he reported that, "The sick were left with plenty of medicines, thirty days' provisions, and the care of a good surgeon and plenty of nurses."[23] This confirms that there existed several sick soldiers, but how many? A clue is contained in the *Cincinnati Commercial* newspaper which states in its October 9, 1862, edition that, "A very large number of the troops here are almost entirely without either socks, shoes, drawers, shirts, or pants. For the last two months a great many of the men have been compelled to go barefoot and in their drawers."[24] The most significant clue comes from the Memoirs of Paul Grogger. He writes in his diary, just one day prior to the evacuation of the Gap on September 17, 1862 that, "All those that was able to march fell in their ranks and those that was not able was left in the hospitals, which was quite a number."[25] How many was "quite a number?" According to the Cincinnati Daily Commercial, 300 sick troops were left behind at Cumberland Gap. According to an earlier edition of the Cincinnati Daily Commercial, Morgan left 500 sick men.[26] It is safe to say that 300-500 men too sick to travel were left when Morgan evacuated the Gap.

The summer of 1862 was very difficult for the troops at the Gap. Sickness ravaged the men and, to compound their misery, one of the worst droughts in years left them parched with thirst.[27] Despite all of these adversities, the men of the 7th Division prepared the Gap for a Confederate attack. Under the leadership of Captain W. F. Patterson, they built a large storehouse capable of storing supplies for 20,000 men for six months.[28] Unfortunately, Morgan was unable to stock it with the necessary supplies. The troops constructed magazines, storehouses for explosives, and other structures to service the army.[29]

Morgan did not overlook training for his officers and men. He appointed Colonel De Courcy and Captain Joseph Edgar, later killed at Tazewell, to teach tactics to the officers of the Tennessee troops.[30] Cumberland Gap was a beehive of activity during the summer of 1862.

VIEW OF CUMBERLAND GAP FROM THE SOUTH, SEPTEMBER 14, 1862. A, Battery No. 1; B, Battery No. 2; C, Fort McClellan; D, Battery No. 3; E, Fort Halleck; 1, 1st Tennessee Regt.; 2, 2nd Tennessee; 5, 49th Indiana; 6, 14th Kentucky; 8, Headquarters Provost Guard; 9, 3d Kentucky; 10, 33rd Indiana; 11, General Baird's Headquarters; 12, General Carter's Headquarters; 13, House used as General Morgan's Headquarters.

Picture taken from Battles and Leaders of the Civil War, Volume III.

Chapter 5
The Case for Invading Kentucky in 1862

Some military historians have criticized Confederate Generals Smith and Bragg for being duped by General John Hunt Morgan, C.S.A., into believing that hordes of Kentuckians would join the Confederate ranks just as soon as Confederate troops invaded Kentucky. During his July 1862 raid, Colonel John H. Morgan sent a message to Kirby Smith advising him that, "the whole country can be secured, and 25,000 or 30,000 men will join you at once."[1] In fact, after the July 1862 raid, Morgan sent Smith a report telling him, "My reception at this place [Harrodsburg] was very encouraging. The whole population appeared to turn out and vie with each other as to who should show us the most attention."[2] In the same report Morgan said, "The people of Georgetown also welcomed us with gladness and provided my troops with everything that they needed."[3]

Historian James Lee McDonough states in his book *War in Kentucky*, "The flamboyant Morgan did not know what he was talking about. Morgan's personal charisma, plus mounting discontent with the Union government in Kentucky, had misled the raider into thinking that the Confederacy enjoyed widespread support."[4] Generals Bragg and Smith were intelligent men. How could they have been so easily misled into believing that Kentuckians would take up arms against the Union? What was the nature of the "mounting discontent" with the Federal Government? What other factors contributed to these two Confederate generals making such a gross error in judgment?

Kentucky became a state in 1792. By 1800, Kentuckians loved the Union so much that, "Patriotic love for the Union now became the keynote of their orators, and anyone so rash as to support sentiments to the contrary was ostracized and even prosecuted."[5] Kentuckians also believed in state rights as much as any Southern state. Almost fifty years earlier Henry Clay held the Federal Government together with compromises through crisis after crisis.[6] In 1849 a national crisis developed in Washington, D.C. over the extension of slavery into California and New Mexico. Clay crafted the Great Compromise of 1850 in which California came into the Union as a free state, and New Mexico and Utah could decide if they were slave states by popular vote.[7] During the debates at Washington, Clay said, "If Kentucky tomorrow unfurls the banner of resistance, I never will fight under that banner. I own a paramount allegiance to the whole Union; a subordinate one to my own state."[8] The State echoed Clay's sentiment by sending a block of Kentucky marble to Washington to be used in the construction of the Washington monument with these words chiseled onto it: "Under the auspices of Heaven and the precepts of Washington, Kentucky will be the last to give up the Union."[9] Kentuckians also believed that they were responsible for solving their own problems and determining their own destiny at the state level. In effect, Kentuckians believed that the rights reserved to the states under the Tenth Amendment of the U.S. Constitution could coexist with a strong Federal Government. This Amendment gave each state the authority to pass laws in areas left unregulated by the Federal government. Southern states, including Kentucky, considered slavery one issue that was reserved to the states under the Tenth Amendment for self-determination.

Slavery existed in the South as a well-entrenched institution. In fact, the entire Southern economy was based on slavery and the labor pool it created. Southern plantation owners owned hundreds of slaves who kept the cotton economy profitable. Thus, the people of the South had a very pragmatic reason for wanting to keep slavery alive — economics. But, "Kentucky was preeminently a land of small slaveholders."[10] "Slavery was, thus, widely dispersed over the state and entrenched with the average Kentuckians, the class that made up the backbone of the state's leadership. The very poor owned few if any slaves; and at the same time many well-to-do Kentuckians did not own slaves — but not necessarily because they disagreed with the institution."[11] So, Kentucky became a land of contrasts. The majority of Kentuckians did not own slaves. Of those who did own slaves, most of them were average Kentuckians. Many of the very poor and the very rich did not own slaves, yet most Kentuckians — poor, rich, slaveholder, and non-slaveholder — believed that they had the right to own slaves if they so desired.

Kentuckians also resented the Northern "do-gooders" who came into the Commonwealth to stir up trouble over the issue of slavery. Religious organizations also kept Kentuckians agitated over slavery.[12] The Presbyterians were particularly active in speaking out against the institution and even assisted in helping to set up and work the Underground Railroad.

Economics, in fact, pulled many Kentuckians toward the South. "From 1820 to the Civil War, constant streams of horses, mules, cattle, and swine passed along the Cumberland Ford route and along other roads to Southern markets."[13] Yet, Kentuckians also had economic ties with the Northern and Eastern markets. The Erie Canal, and later the development of railroads, pulled many Kentucky products into the North. The result of the flow of many Kentucky products to Northern and Eastern markets helped Kentuckians to identify "more with the nation as a whole than absolutely with either section. Here was one of the fundamental forces that was working to make Kentuckians feel neither Northern nor Southern quite so much as American."[14]

Relationships between family and friends also pulled Kentucky toward the Union. By 1860 over 100,000 Kentuckians had moved to Missouri; more than 60,000 had moved to Illinois; 68,000 had moved to Indiana; 15,000 had relocated to Ohio; 13,000 had migrated to Iowa; and 6,000 had moved to Kansas.[15] Few Kentuckians settled in the South. Only Arkansas and Texas received any appreciable number of Kentuckians.[16] Thus, Kentuckians were pulled toward the North as a direct result of more family and friends residing in the Northern states.

Each of these factors left Kentucky paralyzed to make a decision about siding with the North or South. Finally, Kentucky was forced from a position of neutrality to a decision to preserve the Union. Yet, this loyalty to the Union paid the Kentuckians few dividends because Kentucky had one more problem — geography.

Kentucky's unique geographic position in the Union made it necessary for the Union to station thousands of troops in the Bluegrass State during the war. However, these troops treated the Kentuckians like a conquered nation instead of a loyal state. Kentucky entered the war on September 18, 1862 as a loyal Union state.[17] After this declaration to side with the North, Federal officers arrested Kentuckians by the hundreds for simply expressing an opinion sympathetic to the South. "Personal grudges and dislikes were too often the real reason for arrest."[18] On June 1, 1862, General Jere T. Boyle was appointed commander of the Federal forces in Kentucky. Only nine days after his appointment, he began a campaign of arrests on Kentucky citizens that made his name infamous for years. "All persons who had joined the Confederates or who had aided them in any way or had been within their lines were ordered to report to the provost marshals to take the oath of allegiance and to give bond for future good conduct."[19] The Federals let this situation get so out of hand that there just were not enough jails to hold everyone.

Obviously, these conditions created a great deal of animosity toward the "occupying" Union troops. And of course, the Union had good reason to suspect everyone of disloyalty to the Union. By the end of July 1861, fifty companies of Kentuckians joined the Confederacy at Camp Boone that was established on the Tennessee border to accept Kentuckians into the Confederate ranks. Many Kentuckians did side with the South, but the shabby Federal treatment of so many Kentuckians sympathetic to the South drove many Kentuckians into the Confederate camp.[20]

At this time, the Federal Army was in Kentucky to protect it from marauding Confederates. However, it was there also to ensure that the Confederates received no assistance from Kentuckians sympathetic to the South. The Federal military imposed many restrictions on the Kentuckians to achieve these means. After a while, the Kentuckians began to feel that the restrictions were there to punish and harass them. Early in the War, the Federals imposed commercial restrictions designed to control the flow of goods that could assist the Rebel States in their uprising, and the Federals prohibited any commerce in all territory west of the Cumberland River. "Grant, who occupied Paducah in early September (1861), forbade all trade between western Kentucky and Illinois; and shortly thereafter permits were required for all steamers plying west of Louisville."[21] Except in western Kentucky, the boundary line between loyal and disloyal citizens was the Tennessee border.[22]

Nevertheless, many Kentuckians found there was plenty of money to be made by selling their goods to the Confederates and patriotism was an insufficient restraint to prevent them from doing so.[23] "By the summer of 1862, the Federal government had decided to move the boundary of the restricted commercial area to the Ohio River and thus Kentucky, as far as her commercial treatment was concerned, became a part of the Confederacy. Louisville was the only point south of the Ohio at which trade might enter without a permit."[24] Any person attempting to ship goods into the restricted state had to describe the nature of the goods being shipped and take an oath of allegiance to the Union along with a denial of ever aiding the Confederacy.[25] Even merchants in towns of less than 20,000 people were not permitted to purchase food over $3,000 per month for resale.[26] None of these commercial restrictions endeared Kentuckians to the Federal cause.

When John H. Morgan invaded Kentucky in July 1862, he accurately reported the warm reception the people gave him in the towns he entered and along the countryside. As E. Merton Coulter observed in his book *The Civil War and Readjustment in Kentucky*, the Bluegrass Region became a "center of Southern sympathies."[27] In his July 1862 Raid, Morgan stayed in the Bluegrass Region and never went into Eastern Kentucky. He pushed north as far as Cynthiana, 50 miles south of Cincinnati.[28] Thus, he never "took the temperature" of any part of Kentucky except the Bluegrass Region for Confederate support. In fact, more Kentuckians supported the North than the South due to economic ties to the North. Obviously, he assumed that the entire state had the same loyalties as the Bluegrass. He was wrong, but his assumption was certainly a reasonable one considering the fractured and tortured state of affairs in Kentucky during the summer of 1862. This assumption had catastrophic results when the Confederate invasion began in August 1862.

Each of these factors contributed to Generals Kirby Smith and Braxton Bragg misjudging Kentucky's response to a Confederate invasion. Their belief that Kentuckians would rise up and join the Confederate ranks seemed to be a reasonable one; however, their mistake occurred in taking the temperature of Kentucky in only the Bluegrass Region without noting the sentiment in the rest of the Commonwealth.

Chapter 6
Confederate Invasion of Kentucky

Many prominent Kentuckians left Kentucky at the beginning of the Civil War and resettled in Confederate held Tennessee. During June 1862, many of them visited General Bragg. They told him that Kentuckians would rise up and join the Confederate ranks if only the Confederate Army would move into Kentucky.[1]

During the month of July 1862, Confederate Colonel John H. Morgan made a raid into central Kentucky. While in Georgetown, he reported to General Smith that Kentuckians would rise up and join the Confederacy. He reported,

> *"I am here with a force sufficient to hold all the country outside of Lexington and Frankfort. These places are garrisoned chiefly with Home Guards. The bridges between Cincinnati and Lexington have been destroyed. The whole country can be secured, and 25,000 and 30,000 men will join you at once. I have taken eleven cities and towns with very heavy army stores."[2]*

Many Kentuckians may have been sympathetic to the Southern cause, but joining the Confederate army and getting shot at was quite another thing. It wasn't that Kentuckians were afraid to join the fighting — the majority of them supported the Union instead of the Confederacy. However, raising 25,000 to 30,000 Confederate soldiers, as the result of an invasion was just wishful thinking on the part of Confederate leaders.   Nevertheless, many of the Confederate leaders developed a case of "Kentucky fever," including Major-General Kirby Smith, commanding the Confederate forces in Eastern Tennessee.[3] On July 7, 1862, he directed his Aide-de-Camp to write a letter to Brig. Gen. C. L. Stevenson who commanded one of Smith's divisions. He asked Stevenson "to make careful inquiries and get all the information you can with reference to the practicability of moving such a force through Big Creek Gap or by any other route which you may think most practicable."[4] Smith was contemplating moving an army of 10,900 men over Rogers and Big Creek Gaps to invade Kentucky.

On July 24, 1862, Smith sent a letter to Bragg suggesting that there was still time left in the summer to conduct a campaign in Kentucky. Smith promised cooperation when he stated, "I will not only cooperate with you, but will cheerfully place my command under you subject to your orders." [5] Smith made a very large concession to Bragg with his offer to place all Confederate troops in Tennessee under General Bragg's command. Bragg accepted the offer stating that he was "embarrassed in my present position but for the cordial manner in which you have offered cooperation, and indeed placed your command at my disposition. Neither of us have any other object than the success of our cause. I am satisfied no misunderstanding can occur from necessary Union of our forces."[6] These two Confederate generals needed this command structure because they were contemplating entering a hostile land that they thought was friendly. Coordinated action was necessary and could only be achieved through unity of command.

On July 31, 1862, Smith met with Bragg at Chattanooga. They discussed strategy of how best to deal with Union General Buell who was leading his army to Chattanooga. They agreed on a strategy of "mutual support and effective cooperation."[7] In effect, they agreed that Smith would move in front of Cumberland Gap forcing Union General Morgan to abandon it. Even by August 1, 1862, Bragg suspected that General George Morgan was having supply problems at Cumberland Gap because of the poor roads.[8] Once the Gap was securely in Confederate hands, they would combine forces and cut off General Buell, who would be stranded in Middle Tennessee.[9]

Smith must have made a convincing case to Bragg to enter Kentucky with their combined armies when they met in Chattanooga. J. Stoddard Johnston, a Kentucky native and staff officer to General Bragg, also met with General Bragg in Chattanooga sometime during the summer of 1862.[10] Johnston stated in his diary that General Bragg told him he was "massing troops from Alabama to Chattanooga, and he was very glad to see me as he knew nothing of the state, its routes, and topography." [11] General Bragg apparently began to believe also that invading Kentucky, to raise an army, was a good idea.

On August 11, 1862, Smith sent two dispatches to General Bragg. In the first one he stated,

I will move at once with my troops to carry out the plan agreed upon between us, and I deem it almost superfluous to say that I will make no movement that your judgment does not sanction. [12]

In the second dispatch to General Bragg, Smith stated,

I will move as quickly as possible and take position in Morgan's rear where I expect to be by next Sunday evening. Should he have evacuated the Gap I will of course follow him and fight him wherever I can find him. Otherwise I will remain in position in his rear until you think I can move rapidly upon Lexington. I would, however, give it as my opinion that every moment we delay will lessen the great advantages to be gained by an immediate move upon Lexington. General Marshall, with whom I have had a per-

sonal interview, is by this time moving toward Piketon, Morgan County, Ky., with about 3,000 men.[13]

Smith set his sights on Barbourville, Kentucky, as a "position in Morgan's rear." This would place Smith in a position to cut off supplies Morgan received from central Kentucky. However, Smith was only paying "lip service" to Bragg when he said he would follow Morgan and fight him wherever he could find him. Instead of trying to interdict Morgan's supplies, Smith headed straight for Lexington. Smith gave a hint of this independent conduct when he suggested to Bragg that there were "great advantages to be gained by an immediate move upon Lexington." Thus, Smith violated the "unity of command" principle of war, making coordinated efforts and massing of the Confederate troops impossible. This behavior would later have catastrophic results for the Confederate invasion.

Smith sent a letter to Confederate President Jefferson Davis revealing his true intentions with respect to a move towards Lexington on the same day, August 11, 1862, when he pledged to follow General George Morgan at Cumberland Gap no matter where he withdrew. Smith stated in the letter that he would position his army behind Morgan; then, Morgan would most likely respond by moving into central Kentucky. Smith then stated, "If I find he [General George Morgan] has abundant stores two plans present themselves — to invest his position regularly or to move into Kentucky. The latter is, in my mind, the true policy, and I have urged upon General Bragg his consent to my adopting it."[14] Obviously, Smith expected General George Morgan to withdraw from Cumberland Gap along the Pound Gap-Mount Sterling road to Lexington. Smith could then cut Morgan off somewhere in central Kentucky.

To set the trap, on August 11, 1862, Smith ordered General Humphrey Marshall, a West Point graduate, lawyer, and veteran of the Mexican War, to start moving toward Piketon with 3,000 troops to intercept Morgan as he withdrew from the Gap.[15 & 16] Later, Smith would order Marshall to take up a position at Mount Sterling and intercept George Morgan as he traveled along the Pound Gap-Mount Sterling road.

On August 14, 1862, General Smith started for Rogers Gap with 6,000 men. General Henry Heth started from Big Creek Gap with 4,000 men headed for Barbourville. Colonel John S. Scott led 900 cavalry as the eyes and ears of the 10,000 infantrymen.[17] The invasion was on!

By August 16, 1862, Smith's column passed through Rogers Gap.[18] It was a difficult march for the Confederate troops. N. B. Brewer of Company K, 47th Tennessee Infantry Regiment, C.S.A. recorded in his diary of the march, "We were ordered to take up the line of march this morning at 1, o'clock we climed the highest peaks of the Cumberland Mountains to day. Travailed Twenty six miles. Nothing to eat but Rostenyears and Beaf without Sault. The Rougest Road I ever saw [and we] struck the Kentucky Line [and] struck camp for the night."[19]

Morgan was aware that the Confederates had passed through Big Creek Gap and thus pulled in units of his army from Barbourville and Cumberland Ford. However, Morgan overestimated the size of the Rebel army believing that 30,000 Confederate soldiers were on their way to, "attack and surround us."[20] Actually, there were only approximately 10,900 soldiers, most of whom went to Barbourville. Still, that was a force large enough to inflict mortal damage on Morgan.

On the morning of August 16, 1862, Morgan ordered Captain Martin with a small force to observe Big Creek and Rogers Gaps. The next day they were attacked by Confederate cavalry and lost 60 men. The small Union force gathered as much intelligence as possible before limping back to Cumberland Gap. Morgan declared he would hold out at Cumberland Gap as long as he had food and supplies in hopes that Union troops from Lexington would clear the Pound Gap-Mount Sterling road.[21]

On the same day, August 16, 1862, Confederate General Carter Littlepage Stevenson, another West Point graduate, moved the 1st Division comprised of 9,000 troops to a position just south of Cumberland Gap.[22] Stevenson's troops sealed off any retreat for Morgan into Tennessee. Stevenson could then pursue Morgan if he abandoned Cumberland Gap.

On August 18, 1862, Smith entered Barbourville.[23] He remained there until August 26, 1862, when he headed towards Lexington. But why did he leave Barbourville after telling Bragg he would stay and root out Morgan at Cumberland Gap?

First, there were not very many people in Barbourville who could join the Confederate army. Since Smith was looking for troops to join the Confederacy, he needed to go to areas of greater population.

Second, Smith was unable to find any provisions to feed, clothe, and arm his army at Barbourville.[24] Private Sam Thompson of the 1st Texas Battery, who was with Smith as they crossed Big Creek Gap, recorded in his diary, "The country is mountainous and sparsely settled by poor people who have but little to subsist an army on. We are now short of rations." [25] Smith could stay at Barbourville and wait until Morgan's troops ran out of food, but he would be unable to recruit any Kentuckians into the Confederate army. Besides, Smith really didn't know how much food and supplies Morgan had stored up at Cumberland Gap. Smith believed that he could deal with Morgan if he abandoned the Gap wherever he found him with the blocking force of Humphrey Marshall and other Confederate units. Apparently, Smith never considered General Morgan going through Eastern Kentucky a realistic option if Morgan abandoned the Gap. By August 16, 1862, Stevenson was in position in front of Cumberland Gap to pursue Morgan should he choose to retreat.

For General Morgan, things couldn't seem to get any worse, but they did! Smith "sent two divisions, under the command of Major General McCown, to occupy Cumberland Ford."[26] Morgan was now completely sealed off with nowhere to run and he knew it. In his report of October 12, 1862, after he was safely in Ohio, he stated:

We were now closely enveloped by two armies, numbering 45,000 men, and our supplies were entirely cut off. In consequence of bad roads and want of proper transportation our subsistence stores were short, and I immediately placed my command on half rations, with the determination of holding out to the last extremity. [27]

In truth General Morgan was surrounded by approximately 20,000 men; however he was still clearly on the defensive.

On or about September 2, 1862, the 7th Division ran out of flour, which meant they had no bread.[28] Morgan knew his troops had to be fed, so he sent De Courcy's brigade to Manchester hoping to find flour, bacon, and other supplies.[29] De Courcy found hardly enough food for his own brigade, much less for the rest of the Division.[30] Morgan later wrote after the War, "We were destitute of forage. The horses of the 9th Ohio Battery literally starved to death, and their skeletons were dragged outside the lines."[31]

Likewise, General Smith wasn't having much better luck feeding his own invading troops. On August 26, 1862, he led his army, including the two divisions under McCown, to Lexington, satisfied that Barbourville had nothing to help resupply his men.[32] Along the way he encountered Union resistance at Richmond on August 30, 1862, but a fierce battle left the green Union troops scurrying for Louisville.[33]

After the Battle of Richmond, Morgan knew that he would receive no outside assistance. [34] Still Morgan determinedly held on to Cumberland Gap. On September 10, 1862, Morgan sent 200 chosen men from the 1st and 2nd Tennessee Volunteers to Rogers Gap to seal it off under the command of Lieut. Col. M. L. Phillips. Morgan also sent 400 chosen men from Spears' brigade to Big Creek Gap under the command of a Colonel Cooper.[35] These two units killed 30 of the Confederate stragglers, wounded many more, and took 230 prisoners.[36] After being surrounded, Morgan continued to resist, sending 4,000 men on various expeditions, harassing the Confederates at every opportunity.[37]

By August 18, 1862, General George Morgan believed that Union forces in Lexington would come to the aid of the 7th Division defending Cumberland Gap. All he had to do was just hold out with dogged determination. Good military commanders always remain calm in the midst of a crisis and inspire the troops to do their duty. On August 18, 1862, General George Morgan sent the following message to his men.

"Officers and Soldiers of the 7th Division! The opportunity you have so long desired has at length arrived, and you will now prove to your friends, your country and the world that you are soldiers in fact and deed, as well as in name.

The famished enemy is in despair. Driven from Chattanooga, and Richmond escaping from his grasp, he sees that he is forced to occupy Kentucky, Indiana and Ohio, or give up the contest. Two months ago today he ignominiously abandoned this formidable stronghold, although, the force was then greater than yours. If it was then strong, it is infinitely stronger now — stronger in fortifications, stronger in artillery, and, above all, stronger in the brave hearts and strong hearts and strong arms which defend this mountain fortress, destined to become immortal from your glorious deeds.

They talk of the enemy's numbers. Believe me, soldiers, his very strength is his greatness weakness, for the more men he has, the sooner will they starve.

One word to you, and regard that word as fixed as fate. You can

hold this position against any odds, and you have but to determine to con-
quer, and victory is yours!

Comrades, I greet and salute you!

George W. Morgan,

Brigadier-General Commanding the Victors of Cumberland Gap." [38]

By September 3, 1862, a correspondent with the *Cincinnati Daily Gazette* reported from the Gap the condition of the men. He stated "Our boys are active in gathering up fruit, corn, & etc., to make the half rations savory and sufficient. Every man is yet cheerful and hopeful and ready to strike at the enemy whenever he may show himself. All are anxious to have the war honorably and speedily terminated. To accomplish this they are ready and willing to risk much. In a fair field they feel no hesitation in meeting two to one. I think this is the sentiment of the entire army." [39]

On September 12, 1862, General Kirby Smith ordered Brig. General Humphrey Marshall to come to Paris as quickly as possible.[40] Smith was trying to position Marshall so he could intercept Morgan should he abandon Cumberland Gap. Everything was falling into place for the Confederates, making General Morgan's situation at the Gap worse than ever.

Chapter 7
Preparing for the Chase of George Morgan

Confederate officer, John Hunt Morgan, was born on June 1, 1825, in Huntsville, Alabama, and grew up in Lexington, Kentucky.[1] He entered Transylvania College at Lexington, Kentucky, at the age of 16. However, he managed to stay in Transylvania for only two years before being expelled for boisterous behavior.[2] He served in the Mexican War under the command of General Zachary Taylor and performed well as a soldier at Buena Vista in 1847.[3] After the war, he returned to Kentucky and manufactured hemp used to make rope.[4] He stayed inter-

General John Hunt Morgan, *Courtesy Hunt-Morgan House, Lexington, KY*

ested in military service while in Lexington by equipping out of his own pocket the "Lexington Rifles", a militia company. [5]

John Hunt Morgan served as a cavalry squadron commander during the Battle of Shiloh. After witnessing the destruction of close combat with the newest military weapons, he adopted tactics of mobility, surprise, and stealth.[6] During the Civil War, cavalry was primarily utilized for reconnaissance purposes; however, early in the war, they were sometimes utilized for shock purposes much like the modern tank of today. Cavalrymen used sabers as they charged toward an enemy trying to scare him, resulting in the enemy breaking ranks and running in confused retreat. Morgan rejected this concept and armed his horsemen with rifles and pistols instead of the saber.[7] Most of the time he dismounted his troopers and had them fight as infantry.[8]

On July 4, 1862, he began his first of four major raids into Kentucky and Ohio. It was during this raid that he wrote a message to General Kirby Smith advising him that Kentucky could produce between 25,000 to 30,000 soldiers if the Confederacy conducted a major invasion in the Bluegrass State.[9] It was on this raid that he used a portable battery, hooking into the telegraph lines, to send bogus messages to deceive the Federals.[10] Morgan returned to Tennessee on August 4, 1862, after the raid.

On August 28, 1862, he received a message from General Kirby Smith to meet him in Lexington on September 2, 1862. On August 29, 1862, he left from Hartsville, Tennessee, leading 900 men back into Kentucky.[11] By September 2, 1862, they reached Houstonville, Kentucky. It was there that they received news of the Confederate victory at Richmond, Kentucky. Morgan was supposed to meet Smith in Lexington on September 2, 1862, but Morgan didn't arrive in Nicholasville, only twelve miles from Lexington, until dusk on September 3, 1862. Morgan made camp and ordered his troopers to clean up for the grand entry on the next morning. The following day one observer wrote:

The wildest joy ruled the hour. The bells of the city pealed forth their joyous welcome, whilst the waving of thousands of white handkerchiefs and tiny Confederate flags attested the gladness and joy of every heart. Such a scene – I shall never look upon its like again! [12]

Morgan and his men dismounted in the Lexington town square. People placed baskets of food, buckets of water, and all sorts of gifts in the town square for Morgan's men. [13]

Morgan had returned home, but the work of recruitment was just beginning.

Kirby Smith was John Hunt Morgan's superior officer. Smith required many soldiers to fill his infantry ranks. However, he recruited barely enough men in the beginning to man an infantry company. [14] Morgan, being a favorite son of Lexington, recruited enough men to swell his cavalry ranks to just a little less than 1600. [15] Colonel Thomas F. Berry, who rode with Morgan, recorded years later that, "Recruits were now coming in to join the army. There was rejoicing and great enthusiasm." [16] Historian Cecil Fletcher Holland described the situation as such:

Morgan hoped for a response that would raise his command from eleven hundred to a division. A surge of enthusiasm was sweeping the Bluegrass, and recruits poured into his brigade. Ladies of the state presented colors to his cavalry, and his recruiting agents were busy day and night enrolling volunteers. Infantry service was not for Kentuckians, to whom horses and riding were as natural as food and drink. Breckinridge, who enlisted at Georgetown on the July raid, obtained Morgan's permission to raise a battalion of four companies. Roy Cluke and D.W. Chenault received authority to recruit regiments, the Eighth and Ninth Kentucky, and Gano was allowed to withdraw his company to form the nucleus of a new regiment for Morgan's command. Other officers were busy forming companies, and Morgan had no trouble whatever in filling up his ranks beyond the limit he could supply. But Kirby Smith and Bragg scarcely obtained enough volunteers for a single regiment.[17]

However, not every resident in Lexington thought the festivities were wonderful. On September 7, 1862, several horses of the local residents disappeared. A correspondent of the *New York Times* was apparently in town covering the events. He reported, "Horse-stealing was their [John Hunt Morgan's men's] favorite amusement, and this General Smith exerted himself to put a stop to." [18] Smith and Morgan argued strenuously, often times resulting in shouting matches, over whether stealing horses should be allowed to continue and to make the guilty parties pay for their infractions. Smith believed that to win the hearts and minds of the Kentuckians, his troops could not steal their horses. Morgan believed that it was a legitimate exercise of the "spoils of war," but only from citizens who were suspected of supporting the Union cause. Even more significant was that the reporter didn't report this event until Nov. 15, 1862, from Philadelphia. This belated reporting was no doubt a testament to the reporter's clandestine presence among thousands of Confederate troops, and the fact that the Battle of Perryville, Kentucky, in early October, overshadowed Morgan's grand entry into Lexington.[19]

One of Morgan's most trusted and competent subordinate commanders was General Richard M. Gano of the Texas Squadron. The Texas Squadron consisted of two companies of Texans when Morgan reached Lexington. By the time Gano left Lexington two weeks later, he had recruited five companies and now had a full cavalry regiment.

Richard Montgomery Gano was born in Bourbon County, Kentucky on June 17, 1830. He graduated from the Louisville

General Richard M. Gano
Texas State Library and Archives Commission

Medical University in 1850 and practiced medicine for eight years in Kentucky and Louisiana. In 1858 he moved to Grapevine Prairie, Texas, where he farmed, raised livestock, and practiced medicine. He gained military experience in Texas where he raised a company of cavalry to chase a Comanche raiding party. He obviously learned from the Comanche, employing their hit and run tactics during the Civil War. In January 1862, he entered the Confederate Army and organized two companies of Texas cavalry. Morgan entered Lexington with these two Texas companies.

During the parade through Lexington, Gano led his command down the street. Suddenly, Gano recognized Mrs. Billy Moore and her daughter, Mary, who were friends of the family when he lived in Russell's Cave, Kentucky, where they attended the same church. "Gano dismounted from his horse, handed his bridle and reins to Lieutenant Wall, his aid, telling him to lead on, and he turned through the crowd to greet his many friends, kissing Mrs. Moore and her daughter Mary, and all ladies in the crowd and thought that they must treat him likewise, and it has never been known now many women he kissed, but Gano took a pain in the back of his neck from so much stooping, and when he returned to his command Lieutenant Wall said to him, 'You had too big a job on, you ought to have commissioned me to have helped you out.' Gano replied, 'For the first time in my life I got tired [of] kissing and took a pain in the back of my neck.'" [22]

On September 19, 1862, Gano and his command were camping on the Moore's farm. Gano's remark about kissing too many ladies got back to Miss Mary Moore and she confronted him about it. Mary let Gano know she had heard that he had made a remark about her that she didn't appreciate. Acting coy, Mary Moore said, "Never mind, sir, I heard what you said." Gano replied, "What could it have been Miss Mary? I certainly said nothing to hurt you." She responded, "You said you got tired kissing the ladies and I was one of them." [23]

Gano was saved from further embarrassment when his father, mother, sister and cousins pulled up to the scene at that moment to visit him. After visiting his family and friends for two hours, a rider rode up with a message from General Smith. Gano read the message as his friends and family asked him what it said. He responded, "I am going out to meet George Morgan from Cumberland Gap."[24] The ladies began to cry. "They all kissed General Gano goodbye, Mary Moore one of the number, although, she had just said two hours before, 'I won't trouble you with another one of my kisses.'"[25]

Kirby Smith ordered Basil Duke with 600 men to go up to the vicinity of Covington to relieve General Heth who was reconnoitering northern Kentucky. As Basil Duke remembered years later in his memoirs, Colonel John Hunt Morgan was ordered to, "take the remainder of the regiment, Gano's squadron, and all the cavalry recruits then organized, to march to the assistance of General Marshall in the Mountains of Eastern Kentucky."[26] This consisted of Gano's and Cluke's regiments and Breckingridge's battalion.[27] John Morgan commanded approximately 900 men on this mission into eastern Kentucky. General Smith tasked Morgan with the mission of finding Union General George W. Morgan, and delay him until Humphrey Marshall, Carter Stevenson and John Morgan could converge and destroy the 7th Division.[28]

Although we will never know for sure, it is interesting to speculate why Smith chose Duke to move into the more populated areas of northern Kentucky with 600 men to conduct reconnoitering operations. Basil Duke, John Hunt Morgan's brother-in-law, had a reputation for being level headed and being a restraining force on John Hunt Morgan.[29] John Hunt Morgan was a free spirit and allowed his men to plunder Kentuckians suspected of supporting the Union. In contrast, General Smith believed that his troops should restrain themselves and not steal from and infuriate the civilians. As mentioned earlier, Morgan and Smith got into a shouting match when Morgan allowed his cavalry troopers to plunder the civilians in Lexington. What better way to keep Morgan from infuriating the Kentuckians than by sending him to eastern Kentucky where there were fewer populated areas, and thus, fewer civilians to infuriate?

Gen. Smith was unconcerned that Gen. George W. Morgan would turn west and pursue him into central Kentucky. Smith outnumbered the Union forces under George Morgan by a margin of almost two to one counting Carter Stevenson's 9,000 Confederate troops on the south side of Cumberland Gap. If General George Morgan's 7th Division pursued General Smith's Confederate troops into central Kentucky, it would have been suicide for Morgan's army without food or supplies.

Humphrey Marshall's 3000 troops at Mt. Sterling and Morgan's 900 cavalrymen were quite adequate to keep George W. Morgan from being much of a factor in central Kentucky. Smith figured that even if Gen. John Hunt Morgan pillaged the sparse eastern Kentucky countryside in his pursuit of George Morgan, he could not do as much damage to the civilian population as he could in the more populous central Kentucky.

Kentuckians from central Kentucky generally supported the Confederacy; however, Kentuckians from eastern Kentucky generally supported the Union.[30] It made perfect sense to send Morgan into eastern Kentucky where even if he did pillage the eastern Kentuckians, most of them supported the Union anyway. Nothing lost!

On September 19, 1862, Lieutenant E. Cunningham, acting Aid-de-Camp, sent a message at General Smith's request to John Hunt Morgan ordering him to proceed to Irvine, Kentucky, and begin his search for General George W. Morgan. Smith had received a report that George W. Morgan had abandoned Cumberland Gap. John Morgan's job was to confirm this report and keep Smith informed of George Morgan's movements. Smith speculated that if George Morgan had in fact abandoned the Gap, he was headed for Maysville,

Kentucky. If George Morgan had not abandoned the Gap, Smith wanted John Morgan to burn the mills and grain at Manchester since it was on George Morgan's way to either Maysville or any other destination in eastern Kentucky.[31]

George Morgan abandoned Cumberland Gap on September 16, 1862. General Smith sent John Hunt Morgan to find him, delay him, and then destroy him in conjunction with other Confederate units that would be brought to bear on the 7th Division. The hunt was on!

Chapter 8
Confederate Plan to Destroy the 7th Division

On September 10, 1862 Major-General Kirby Smith sent a message to General Humphrey Marshall ordering him to proceed to Cynthiana and Falmouth to support General Heth.[1] Smith sent Heth into northern Kentucky to threaten Cincinnati, tying down more Union troops in that area.[2] It soon became apparent that Heth's troops were not needed in northern Kentucky. Smith ordered Heth and his 4,000 to 5,000 troops and 18 pieces of artillery to proceed to Mt. Sterling to intercept George Morgan, in the event he was trying to reach Maysville via Mt. Sterling.[3] This was a reasonable speculation since Mt. Sterling was at the terminus of the Pound Gap-Mt. Sterling Road. It was the only road out of Eastern Kentucky capable of accommodating rolling artillery, according to conventional thought.

On September 18, 1862, Smith ordered Marshall to proceed to Mt. Sterling, "in order to intercept General Morgan. His forces are completely demoralized, and I think it will be an easy matter for you to capture it." Smith notified Heth that General Marshall had been ordered to cooperate with Heth by meeting him at Mt. Sterling. Smith stressed to Marshall that it was, "of the greatest importance that your command shall. . ." assist General Heth.[4] It seems odd that one general would have to impress upon another general the importance of cooperating with other generals during an invasion. In fact, General Smith sent a message to General Bragg on September 18, 1862, concerning tactical information. In that message Smith stated, "Marshall should advance to Mount Sterling, but I fear he will not come."[5]

Map of The Mount Sterling-Pound Gap Road
http://www.geocities.com

On September 19, 1862, Jefferson Davis himself sent a message to General Humphrey Marshall warning him of the dangers of operating independently. Davis stated, "No one can have an independent command. Cooperation is necessary to success, and the senior officer present for duty must command the whole. It was expected that you would have moved with General Smith into Kentucky."[6] Actually, he didn't begin his move into Kentucky until early September.[7] Smith's concern for Marshall's cooperation was justified. Marshall's lack of assistance would later allow the 7th Division to slip through the fingers of the Confederate vice. What created this uncertainty about Marshall's cooperation?

General Marshall was born in Frankfort, Kentucky on January 13, 1812. His family tree included Chief Justice of the United States Supreme Court John Marshall, who wrote the famous *Marbury vs. Madison* opinion giving Federal courts the right to review the constitutionality of laws passed by Congress. His family also included Kentucky historian Humphrey Marshall, and orator and attorney, Thomas F. Marshall. He had a pedigree and he knew it![8]

In 1833 he graduated from West Point 42nd out of a class of 45.

Brigadier-General
Humphrey Marshall
*Battles and Leaders
of the Civil War, Vol. I*

In 1834 he resigned his commission and studied law. He practiced law in Louisville, Kentucky until the outbreak of the Mexican-American War. He raised a cavalry regiment and fought with distinction in Mexico during the battle of Buena Vista in February 1847.[9]

Marshall practiced law in Kentucky before the War. His pedigree and war record helped him become a U.S. Representative from 1849 to 1852. Additionally, from 1852 to 1854, he served as U.S. minister to China. Upon returning to the United States, he served in the U.S. House of Representatives from 1855 to 1859.[10] After the southern states seceded in early 1861, he continued to insist that neutrality was the best policy for Kentucky. Finally, he accepted a commission in the Confederate Army as a brigadier general after realizing that Kentucky would not be allowed to remain neutral much longer.[11] His troubles began when he cast his lot with the Confederacy.

On March 19, 1862, Marshall wrote a letter to General Robert

E. Lee complaining of his, "dissatisfaction with the current state of affairs."[12] Marshall was made commander of the Army of Eastern Kentucky and promised 5,000 men. What Marshall really received was an army on paper. He had to raise his own troops. To make matters worse, he had competition for recruiting troops from the Union as well. He advised Lee that Virginian troops were reluctant to fight in Kentucky. He even went on to advise Lee that the "proposed invasion of Kentucky by General Kirby Smith would be a mistake." [13]

One other problem contributed to Marshall's woes. The enlistment period for the 5th Kentucky Infantry, a significant part of his force, was only for one year. As they enlisted in early October 1861, many of Marshall's troops' enlistments expired in October 1862. Many of his men wanted to stay in Kentucky yet get out of Confederate service at the end of their enlistments.[14] Thus, many of Marshall's troops were not "itching" for a fight so close to being discharged from service.

Marshall's lack of disciple toward his men also played a factor in his reluctance to cooperate with the rest of the Confederate invading force. He was not "qualified to command volunteers, being the most democratic of men. Moreover, his heart was tender as a woman's. For these reasons he could not enforce the rigorous discipline of an army."[15] Marshall's leniency made control of his troops problematic. One of his staff officers offered to eat the first man that Marshall would shoot for any crime.[16] At the end of the invasion when the Confederate troops pulled back into Tennessee, the Union Army dispatched forces to eastern Kentucky to stop Marshall's men from, "committing outrages upon the people and depredations upon their property." [17] It is most likely that "Marshall's men" were the Confederates who elected to stay in Kentucky when their enlistments expired in early October 1862. Kentucky was fertile ground for criminals to steal, plunder, and pillage the countryside so as to "line their own pocketbooks", all in the name of the Confederacy.

In Kirby Smith's message to Marshall of September 18, 1862, Smith told Marshall to concentrate his force at Mount Sterling, "in order to intercept General Morgan. His forces are completely demoralized, and I think it will be an easy matter for you to capture it."[18] Smith clearly indicated an intention for Marshall to combine forces with General Heth at Mount Sterling. This gave the Confederates a combined force at Mount Sterling of approximately 8,000 troops and 20 pieces of artillery. Later, on September 24, 1862, Smith notified Marshall that General Leadbetter's brigade would be in supporting distance of Mount Sterling if necessary. Leadbetter had 1,600 troops. Thus, 9,600 Confederate troops were massing at Mount Sterling for the expected interception of George Morgan's 7th Division. Smith was properly applying the military principle of mass. Smith figured that once Morgan left Cumberland Gap, Marshall and the massed 9,600 troops could block him, thus preventing his escape. General Stevenson, with his 9,000 troops on the south side of Cumberland Gap, could pursue Morgan and slam in behind him as the massed forces at Mount Sterling blocked their retreat. Smith figured that he could bring his 10,900 troops to bear at Mount Sterling at the same time resulting in the destruction of the 7th Division.[19] This is a classic military maneuver known as the hammer and anvil. The massed troops at Mount Sterling would act as the anvil holding Morgan's forces in check while Smith and Stevenson's forces hammered them from the rear and side. The strategy was sound, but as often occurs in war—commanders need to be flexible because the enemy doesn't always conduct their movements according to commanders' plans.

Chapter 9
Cumberland Gap-Fall 1862

General George Morgan knew that Confederate troops were massing in Tennessee in early August 1862 for a possible invasion into Kentucky. He also knew that the 7th Division was in a precarious place trying to defend Cumberland Gap. Morgan knew that he would lose the Gap unless he could store enough supplies to last at least a year. General John Coburn of the 33rd Regiment of Indiana recalled years later that

It is safe to say that had three months supplies for 80,000 men been deposited in Cumberland Gap, Smith would not have invaded Kentucky in the fall of 1862. He would never have dared to leave the line of the Virginia and Tennessee Railroad, as it was left comparatively defenseless.

When these armies got in our rear we had but a scanty supply of provisions and feed for a few days. It was impossible to lay up a store. The evacuation of Cumberland Gap was a necessity, with starvation or surrender staring in the face of 10,000 men, under Gen. Morgan, of Ohio. Greater armies occupied the attention of the authorities at Washington, but a greater opportunity never was offered at a smaller cost during that eventful time.[1]

On August 8, 1862, Morgan telegraphed Captain Brown, assistant quartermaster in Lexington, pleading for supplies. Morgan stated that, "Twenty-five thousand men are between this place and Knoxville, and they are constantly arriving by way of Dalton. The safety of this place depends upon the supplies, which you can rush forward. Not a second is to be lost. Give us supplies and we will be regardless of the enemy's force."[2] On August 10, 1862, Morgan telegraphed General Buell stating that he had, "about three weeks' supplies for my entire command."[3] Shortly after August 16, 1862, when the Confederate invasion began, General George Washington Morgan placed his Division on half rations, except beans and rice.[4]

General Smith figured that trying to storm the Gap would be too costly in men. So, the rebels settled for a strategy of attrition against Morgan and the 7th Division. Smith severed Morgan's supplies, so it was only a matter of time before Morgan would have to surrender. By September 5, 1862, Morgan ran out of flour to bake bread.

On September 8, 1862, Morgan ordered DeCourcey's Brigade and Capt. Foster's Battery, 1st Wisconsin, to march to Manchester, Clay County, Kentucky. Morgan sent DeCourcy's Brigade to Manchester for three reasons. First, it would be four thousand (4000) less men to feed at the Gap. Second, the Brigade could look for food and send it back to the Gap. Third, the Brigade could provide an advanced guard for the rest of the Division if Morgan ordered the evacuation. "On leaving the Gap, his [DeCourcey's] Brigade had drawn three biscuits per man, to serve as five days rations, and when corn and sour apples failed they fell back upon paw-paws, the one natural product of that desolate country which could sustain human life."[5]

DeCourcey's Brigade took only 48 hours to cover the approximately 50 miles. They arrived at Manchester on September 10th at 8:00 A.M. where they made camp one mile from the town. At sundown they immediately took up defensive positions on the hilltop between their camp and the town. DeCourcey deemed it necessary to take up these defensive positions because John H. Morgan and his Confederate cavalry continued to harass the Union troops. On September 12, 1862, Dr. Benjamin Stevenson of the 22nd Kentucky Infantry wrote in his diary, "I understand we wait here [Manchester] for the coming up of Gen. George W. Morgan."[6] General Morgan had not yet assembled his staff when he made the decision to withdraw from Cumberland Gap. As much as Dr. Stevenson was supposed to know, Morgan had sent them to Manchester to find food for his men, horses, and mules. Why would Dr. Stevenson believe that Morgan would be coming to Manchester?

Gen. George W. Morgan knew that Smith's arrival in Lexington destroyed any chance of linking up with General Don Carlos Buell coming down from Louisville. [7] Apparently, Morgan contemplated abandoning Cumberland Gap by September 10, 1862, when he sent DeCourcey to secure a base at Manchester. Morgan trusted DeCourcey's judgment and held him in the highest esteem as a military commander. In fact, Morgan recommended that DeCourcey be promoted to a brigadier general, as were the other brigade commanders. Morgan must have shared his thoughts on abandoning the Gap with DeCourcey. Consequently, military scuttlebutt must have filtered down to Dr. Stevenson giving him the idea that they were waiting on Morgan to join them at Manchester.

Morgan kept his men busy continuously hardening the defensive positions. *The Cincinnati Commercial*, a Cincinnati newspaper with a reporter attached to the 7th Division at Cumberland Gap, reported that "the troops appear comparatively cheerful, and day after day perform heavy picket duty and labor at the defenses. As I write, a thousand or more picks and shovels are working away at mother earth. Stronger and stronger grows the place, and more haggard and gaunt grow the troops."[8] By September 11, 1862, their corn was gone and their supply of beans and rice was nearly exhausted.

The troops' clothes became another issue as they literally wore them out while at the Gap. *The Cincinnati Commercial* reporter wrote, "A very large number of the troops here are almost entirely without either socks, shoes, drawers, shirts, or pants. For the last two months a great many of the men have been compelled to go barefoot, and in their drawers."[9] The situation grew bleaker each day.

Private Owen Johnston Hopkins of Company K, 42nd Regiment, Ohio Volunteer Infantry, stated in his diary that,

Our supplies grew shorter day by day, and even the horses and mules of the army were failing for want of forage. Morgan would not stir from his position, declaring that he would kill the horses and mules for food, did he see any movement set on foot to open his communications.

The country was alarmed for our safety. The very stubbornness with which he held the grim fortress, only insured our total destruction, if no relief should reach us. We were put on half-rations a good part of the time, without bread, flour, or potatoes. The overwhelming enemy continued to draw closer and closer around us every day, narrowing our field for forage until, at length, starvation began to stare us in the face. The men looked lank and haggard from hunger and exposure, and were almost worn out by arduous duties in the chill mountain air at night, and as no man amongst the privates possessed a full suit of clothing, suffering from cold was added to that of hunger.[10]

Morgan's 7th Division was going without food and clothing because the Confederates had severed Morgan's supply line coming out of central Kentucky. Morgan's troops were so cut off from the rest of the states that they heard about the Union loss at Manassas from a Confederate newspaper that came into the Gap during a prisoner exchange.[11]

A short time earlier, the Federal War Department reorganized the Department of the Ohio placing Union Major General Horatio G.

Wright in command of all Union forces located in Kentucky. This created a confusing chain of command. Nevertheless, on September 9, 1862, Morgan wrote a letter to Maj. Gen. Wright, who was located at Cincinnati, Ohio. General Wright was General Buell's commander and Buell was, of course, Morgan's commander. In the military then and today, it is taboo to jump the chain of command. However, Morgan did just this by writing the letter directly to General Wright. Apparently, Morgan was dissatisfied with Buell's response to the 7th Division's needs at Cumberland Gap. Later, this gave Morgan's critics more ammunition during the Buell inquiry. Morgan stated in the letter that he thought he had enough supplies to hold out at Cumberland Gap 60 more days if two events occurred: if Col. DeCourcy's brigade succeeded in locating sufficient flour and bacon at a mill located in Manchester, Kentucky, and if the remaining men at Cumberland Gap ate their mules. If these two events occurred, Morgan reported to General Wright he thought he could hold out sixty more days.[12]

Lt. Col. Munday's cavalry screening the 7th Division's column. Picture taken by Lewis D. Nicholls at reenactment celebrating John Morgan's Raiders near Pomeroy, Ohio, October 2003.

Morgan sent one of his aides-de-camp, Lt. Charles S. Medary, to deliver the message to General Wright. Lt. Medary left on September 10, 1862, to take the message to General Wright. On the way to Cincinnati, Medary went through Manchester and found DeCourcy. Decourcy told Medary that the only food he found was barely adequate to feed his own Brigade, much less the entire Division.[13] Of course, Morgan had no way of knowing that DeCourcy had been unsuccessful in locating sufficient flour and bacon at Manchester when he wrote the letter to General Wright. Medary arrived at Cincinnati on September 17, 1862, and advised General Wright that he did not believe the defenders at the Gap could hold out for more than 20 to 30 days.[14]

George Morgan's route with 7th Div. through Eastern KY wilderness
Battles and Leaders of the Civil War, III

Morgan finally decided that to stay at the Gap any longer would insure the capture or destruction of the 7th Division. Consequently, on September 14, 1862, he assembled his Brigade commanders and several members of his staff. Brigadier-Generals Spears, Baird, and Carter, Lieutenant Craighill as recorder, and Captain Sidney S. Lyon as topographical engineer were all present. The only brigade commander not present was Col. DeCourcy, who was at Manchester trying to locate food. Morgan called this meeting a "council of war", but actually it was a "council of escape and evasion."[15]

This meeting was typical of Morgan's leadership style. He would solicit the opinions of his subordinate commanders and staff and then make the ultimate decision. He asked Captain Sidney S. Lyon, a geologist who had surveyed parts of eastern Kentucky before the war, "Can I take my division by that route to the Ohio River?"[16] Morgan lined out a route on the map through Manchester, Booneville, West Liberty, Grayson and Greenupsburg (Greenup) located on the Ohio River. Lyon replied, "Yes, possibly, by abandoning the artillery and wagons."[17] Lyon knew that this proposed route followed an old Indian "Warriors' Path" and in many places was no more than a mere path even then.[18]

Morgan prudently sent Lieutenant-Colonel George W. Gallup, of the 14th Kentucky, on a reconnoiter of the proposed route. The men in the 14th were familiar with the route and reported that several factors discouraged following it. First, they reported that there was little water along the proposed route. Second, they reported that the steep mountains made taking this route very difficult. Third, they reported that a few wagons, with no more than a half-ton on each wagon might get through.[19] Morgan figured that if he retreated to Lexington it would place the 7th Division, with its diminished effective fighting ability, between Smith on his front, Bragg on his left, and Humphrey Marshall on his right.[20] A retreat to Lexington was certain destruction. Morgan's only chance of survival for the 7th Division was along the route of the Indian "Warrior's Path."

General Morgan never let the brigade commanders know that he thought Cumberland Gap should be abandoned. Instead, he let each of the brigade commanders express his opinion about what should be done about the situation. After a thorough consultation, they all arrived at the same conclusion—surrender or evacuate.[21] If they surrendered, it meant the loss of 10,000 Union troops. If they evacuated, it meant that 10,000 Union troops would either perish in the wilderness of eastern Kentucky or escape to fight another day. Morgan and his commanders evaluated a third option — stay at Cumberland Gap. This option meant certain starvation for 10,000 Union troops. Morgan decided to evacuate after carefully weighing each of the options. He waited one more day until September 15, 1862, in hopes that word of a relief column was on its way before giving the order to abandon the Gap. None came. Abandoning Cumberland Gap was the only option that Morgan and the 7th Division had for survival. Morgan reported that all of his officers and men agreed with the decision including Generals Spears and Carter from Tennessee.[22]

It was at this point that Morgan ordered Captain George M. Adams, Commissary of Subsistence, to send a young officer with two or three men on a mission of deception. Morgan composed a bogus message authorizing the officer to purchase food for the entire 7th Division.[23] Morgan stated in the message that it was his intention to cross the Ohio River at Maysville, Kentucky. Captain Adams sent the officer and his two or three men towards Maysville, along the Pound Gap-Mt. Sterling Road after the main body reached Manchester. Morgan figured the Confederates would capture the officer, and his detail, along this route. In fact, Morgan counted on it! The Confederates did, in fact, capture the small detachment and they studied the bogus message. Smith bought the ruse!

As a result of the intercepted message, General Smith issued orders from September 18 to September 24, 1862, to mass the troops of Generals Marshall, Heth, and Ledbetter, totaling 9,600 troops near Mt. Sterling. Even after General John Hunt Morgan found the 7th Division in the eastern Kentucky wilderness, Marshall refused to leave his Mt. Sterling position and intercept Morgan near West Liberty. This was a clear indication that Morgan's ruse was effective! As a result of this deception, the 7th Division never encountered any resistance along the evacuation route through eastern Kentucky other than the 900 cavalry of General John Hunt Morgan.

Gen. George W. Morgan once again demonstrated his sound generalship with this deception by applying the principle of security and surprise. Morgan's ruse confused the Confederates long enough to give the 7th Division an opportunity for escape from certain destruction through the wilderness of eastern Kentucky.

Chapter 10
Evacuation of Cumberland Gap

On September 15, 1862, Morgan gave the command for abandonment of Cumberland Gap. Morgan ordered Capt. W. F. Patterson
to mine the road and mountainsides of the Gap. Capt. Patterson ordered Lieut. W. P. Craighill, who was an army engineer by training,
to mine the road and mountainsides. [1] Morgan hoped that the explosion would cause part of the mountainside to slide down, blocking
the road. Lt. Craighill also mined the magazines and store-houses.[2]
Morgan intended to burn very building that could be of any use to
the Confederates.

Morgan also decided to save as many artillery guns as possible. He had thirty-two artillery pieces, and four of them were 30-
pound pieces. The 30-pounders were too large to move by horses, so
Morgan ordered Captain Tidd, a mechanic of the telegraph corps, to
spike only the 30-pounders. [3] The Union soldiers then pushed the 30-
pounders over the cliffs.[4] The remaining lighter artillery pieces were
then hitched to teams of horses ready to evacuate. Six of these remaining artillery pieces were 20-pounders. The rest of them were most
likely 12-pounder smoothbores that were mobile horse drawn pieces.
Thomas Speed reported that Morgan ordered nine "siege guns de-

stroyed."[5] These guns were most likely the large pieces left by the Confederates when they originally abandoned Cumberland Gap back in June 1862.

On September 16, 1862, Morgan sent a large train of wagons on the road to Manchester accompanied by the Thirty-third Indiana, two companies of the Third Kentucky, and the Ninth Ohio Battery. Morgan placed Colonel Coburn under command of the convoy.[6]

Mobile smoothbore artillery piece located at Cumberland Gap, Kentucky. Photograph taken by Lewis D. Nicholls. (Most likely a 20 pound smoothbore horse-drawn artillery piece George Morgan took with him when he abandoned Cumberland Gap on September 17, 1862.)

Sickness took a toll on the men of the 7th Division. Morgan left between 300 and 500 men at the Gap who were too sick to travel with the evacuation. The hot sun, lack of proper hygienic practices, drought, labor to prepare the Gap for possible battle, and troop movements to respond to Kirby Smith's invasion left as many as 1000 men of the 7th Division in a weakened condition as they began their evacuation.[7]

Paul Grogger of the 2ⁿᵈ Tennessee (part of the Union 7ᵗʰ Division) described the evacuation from Cumberland Gap:

"It was dark and drizzly night when we started. All those that was able to march fell in their ranks and those that was not able was left in the hospitals, which was quite a number. It was with much feeling of pity and sorrow that we had to leave them to the mercy of the rebels, especially as we heard afterwards that the rebs came and fell in like hungry hounds and devoured every thing that we left for the sick. They even took most of their blankets and bed clothes.

Twelve pound smooth-bore horse drawn artillery piece. It is the type George Morgan took with him when he abandoned Cumberland Gap, Ky. on Sept. 17, 1862. Photograph taken by Lewis D. Nicholls.

We all made our knapsacks as light as possible and only took the most necessary things of our camp equipage along with us, as we could from all appearances anticipate nothing else but a long and weary march. Yet, few of us knowed where we was a going. Anyhow, we did not get disappointed from our expectation. The march was long and weary and before we got through we went to the Ohio River." [8]

As darkness befell Cumberland Gap on Wednesday night, September 17, 1862, the main body of the 7ᵗʰ Division clandestinely evacuated Cumberland Gap. Morgan placed Lieutenant-Colonel Gallup, provost-marshall of the post, aided by Captain McNeish, to hold the rebels back until the Division could evacuate.[9] Morgan gave Gallup 200 of his best men to accomplish this mission.

Troops from Col. Patterson's Engineers dug a pit approximately 20 square feet and 25 feet deep. Troops lined up on either side of the pit and marched by it in double column. Most of the men were armed with Springfield firearms. The officers ordered the men to throw their Springfield firearms into the pit. Morgan ordered the men to draw new Belgium firearms to replace the Springfields from the temporary armory located in the Headquarters building. The Belgium firearms were longer and heavier, and thus more cumbersome to carry than the Springfields. However, they had approximately 80 rounds per man for the Belgium firearms as compared to only 20 rounds per man for the Springfields. General U. S. Grant said that the Belgium firearms were "almost as dangerous to the person firing them, as to the one aimed at."[10] The men also threw additional equipment, too heavy to carry, into the pit. These additional items included cartridge-boxes, bayonets, tents, 1,000 screwdrivers, 10,000 lbs. of lead, 6,000 lbs. of cannon balls and other paraphernalia of war.[11]

The engineers then set mines, explosive devices, to blow up the pit with the arms and equipment. Morgan had built several magazines, facilities to hold ammunition, during the occupation of the Gap and he ordered them to destroy all munitions in the magazines that they were unable to carry. Gallup positioned five men at each magazine and at the arms pit; they were supposed to ignite the explosive devices and then rejoin the rest of the column. Other men were detailed to set fire to the military storehouse, commissary and quartermaster buildings, tents, and anything else that would be of any value to the rebels.[12]

Morgan reported, "Everything moved with the precision of a well-constructed and well-oiled piece of machinery until late in the afternoon of the 17th, when a report came from our signal station on the crest of the mountain that a flag of truce from the enemy was approaching."[13] The Confederates were unable to actually see the Federal preparation for abandonment of Cumberland Gap because the mountains obstructed their view. Once again Morgan adhered to the principle of security in preparing the Division for evacuation in complete secrecy. Up to this point, Morgan had committed no errors in military judgment.

The Confederates were well aware of Morgan's plight, i.e. no food for his troops and severed supply lines. The Confederates reasonably anticipated that Morgan might have to evacuate the Gap or lose the entire Division. Thus, the Confederates sent a small party to "talk" about possible surrender at dusk on the 17th. In reality, the Confederates were trying to observe the preparations for evacuation to obtain a better picture of the Federal movements.[14]

Morgan responded to this Confederate "observation party" under a flag of truce by sending Lieutenant-Colonel Gallup with a small detail of soldiers and several other officers. The two detachments met at dusk on the south side of Cumberland Gap. They engaged in light-hearted verbal jousting with each other for about an hour. As the two enemies teased each other in this surreal scene, suddenly a glare of fire and smoke appeared over the Poor Valley Ridge. One Confederate said, "Why, Colonel, what does that mean? It looks like an evacuation." The quick-witted Gallup quickly responded, "Not much. Morgan has cut away the timber obstructing the range of his guns, and they are now burning the brush on the Mountain-side." This explanation was consistent with what the Confederates had observed ever since the Federals had occupied the Gap at the beginning of the summer.[15] The two enemies parted company with Gallup telling the Confederate officer that he would see him in the morning and they could further discuss the issue of surrender.[16] Lt. Col Gallup then visited his pickets guarding the approaches through the Gap. He told them to dispute every inch of ground. He then went to Morgan's headquarters. [17] He found General Morgan sitting on his horse observing the retiring columns headed towards Cumberland Ford.[18] There he learned that a careless soldier had torched the quartermaster building prematurely. This careless act nearly cost Morgan the element of surprise

During daylight of September 17, 1862, the quartermaster issued the troops, "about 4 pounds of pork or bacon, a few pounds of corn meal or flour and a little salt in their knapsacks, and their blanket roll, for this long march. They got more food along the way when they could — or went without."[19] At 8:00 P.M. that evening, Morgan ordered his remaining troops into a column formation. Morgan reported in his official report to Major General Horatio G. Wright that his men responded "with the coolness and precision of troops on review; and without hurry, without confusion, with no loud commands, but with resolute confidence, the little army, surrounded by peril on every side set out on its march of more than two hundred miles through the wilderness."[20] Morgan ordered Spears brigade in a line formation at the foot of the mountain on the north side of the Gap. He then ordered an element of Foster's battery between the regiments so that each regiment could have supporting artillery if necessary. At midnight Morgan ordered Carter's brigade off the mountain followed by Baird's brigade.[21] Morgan reported that the "descent was slow, difficult, and dangerous."[22]

At 10 p.m., a breathless courier appeared at Morgan's headquarters. The courier told Morgan that a Union sentinel had abandoned his post and defected to the Confederate side.[23] Morgan was sure that surprise of the evacuation had been compromised. All of his heavy artillery except one piece had been withdrawn.[24] The 7th Division was now really in peril because it had no way to defend itself if the Confederates struck.

During the initial phase of the evacuation, Morgan's troops were not in a tactical formation. They were in a column formation designed to move troops quickly along a road. Although a column formation carries with it the feature of moving troops quickly, it leaves the retreating troops vulnerable to attack. If the Confederates believed that Morgan's men were evacuating, then an attack upon a column formation could inflict heavy casualties on the retreating Union troops. Surprise and stealth under the cover of darkness were critical for

Morgan to safely evacuate Cumberland Gap.

Gallup was still with Morgan when they received the report of the defecting sentinel. Gallup and Morgan were each on their horses when Morgan looked at Gallup and said, "You have a highly important duty to perform. This ammunition and these arms and stores must not fall into the hands of the enemy. I hope you will not be captured. Farewell." Morgan then bowed and rode into the darkness to lead his retreating column.[25]

Morgan left Gallup with 200 men to guard the main column's rear as they retreated. When the last man abandoned the Gap, except for the sick left behind, Gallup ordered his detachment of 200 men to march on the road to Cumberland Ford. He then detailed three men, Markham, O'Brien, and Thad Reynolds to ignite the storehouses, commissary, quartermaster buildings, headquarters, and all other structures including tents. Thad Reynolds was reputed to be the "boldest scout and spy in the army."[26] Gallup gave the signal to ignite the structures. Soon the evening sky was reddened with the smoke and illumination of the fires. Gallup then gave the signal to blow up the mountainside and munitions. There was nothing but silence. He waited a reasonable period of time for the explosion to occur. When he heard no explosion, he rode over to the location and found no one there. All of the soldiers had left and joined the main column without igniting the explosive charges. Gallup quickly obtained burning embers and ignited the explosive charges himself. He then rode his horse as fast as possible to escape the explosion. He barely reached a safe distance when the first explosion occurred. Credit can only be given to a description of the next scene as described by Private Owen Johnston Hopkins of the 42nd Regiment, Ohio Volunteer Infantry, as he stated in his diary:

The savage precipices reddened like fire in the sudden illumination, and the whole midnight gorge shone brighter than at midday. One can imagine

Gallup sitting on his horse, that glowed like a fiery steed in the intense glare of the flames, gazing with silent awe on the wild work his hands had wrought, every fissure and opening in the cliffs around him visible. The trees and rocks, at any time picturesque and interesting, now grand in their beauty. It must have been a scene more like enchantment than reality.

But suddenly the scene changed. The large magazine with its stores of fixed ammunition and powder exploded, shaking the mountains like a toy in the hands of a monster. The air was filled with dense smoke and huge masses of rock. Cartridge boxes, barrels of powder and other materials were blown to an incredible height, and went whirling through the air in wild confusion, falling in some instances, it is said, more than a mile from the exploding magazine. A moment after, the roof of a building 180 feet long, used as a storehouse on the mountain, fell in and set fire to the shells stored there. Before the blazing embers that shot in a fiery shower heavenward had descended to the earth again, the explosion took place, sounding like a thousand cannon let off there at once in the trembling gorge.[27]

Lt. Col. Gallup continued to guard the retreating formation with his 200 chosen men further on down the road until nearly dawn. Then, Gallup withdrew his men and they evacuated north continuing to cover the rear of the retreating column.[28]

Paul Grogger of the 2nd Tennessee (Federal) recalled that the night of September 17-18, 1862 was a "dark and drizzly night."[29] This type of night masked the Federal withdrawal. Since the leaves were wet, they did not make the usual cracking sound as troops marched over them alerting the Confederates of the evacuation.

Confederate General Carter L. Stevenson dared not pursue General Morgan and the Federals until 3:00 P.M. the following day, Thursday, September 18, 1862, because of unexploded munitions scattered around the Cumberland Gap area.[30] Of course, with an explosion of this magnitude, the Confederates knew that the Federals had abandoned the Gap.

The Confederates speculated that Morgan was marching to Maysville.[31] Of course, Morgan helped promote this belief by sending the quartermaster officer along the Pound Gap-Mt. Sterling Road with the bogus message for them to purchase supplies for Morgan's army headed toward Maysville.

Morgan's troops marched to Cumberland Ford by morning. Paul Grogger of the 2nd Tennessee recalled that they ate a quick breakfast of hardtack and coffee and rested only long enough to regain their strength.[32] The Federals made no camp, rested only briefly, then continued the march. The column arrived at Flat Lick on Friday evening, September 19, 1862.[33] Flat Lick was approximately twenty miles north of Cumberland Ford. Morgan's column halted at Flat Lick and made their first camp.[34]

The next morning, Saturday, September 20, 1862, Morgan divided his column into two groups where the road diverged at Flat Lick. He sent the first group along the Stinking Creek Road towards Manchester. The second group proceeded along the Goose Creek Road

EVACUATION OF CUMBERLAND GAP
Lithograph taken from The Great Rebellion by J. T. Headley

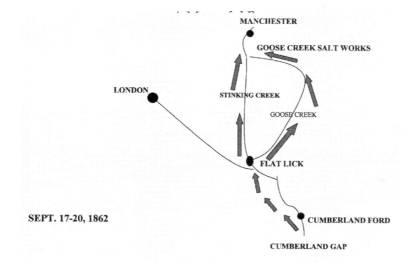

MANCHESTER

GOOSE CREEK SALT WORKS

LONDON

STINKING CREEK

GOOSE CREEK

FLAT LICK

SEPT. 17-20, 1862

CUMBERLAND FORD

CUMBERLAND GAP

Beginning route taken by George Morgan and 7th Division
during evacuation of Cumberland Gap.

also headed towards Manchester via the Goose Creek Salt works. He
divided his column in this manner to make better time along two
parallel roads.[35] Paul Grogger of the 2nd Tennessee proceeded along
the Goose Creek Road headed towards the Goose Creek Salt works
located just south of Manchester. It was on this road that he reported
that some rebel cavalry pursued them, but did not attack. Instead,
the rebels only managed to pick up a few Federal stragglers.[36] The
rebel cavalry was most likely lead elements of Stevenson's pursuit.

On Saturday, September 20, 1862, early in the morning, the
Federal column arrived at Manchester in Clay County.[37] Morgan reorganized his column for the long march towards the Ohio River. He
also rested the fatigued troops all day Saturday. By this time Confederate General Stevenson's troops had made contact with rear elements
of Colonel Cooper's Federal Sixth Tennessee. Morgan reported in his
official report that Cooper's Sixth Tennessee, "gallantly repulsed" the
pursuing Confederate troopers.[38]

Morgan earlier had sent ahead DeCourcey's Brigade to

Manchester on September 8, 1862, to secure food and supplies. DeCourcey's Brigade arrived on September 10, 1862, but were unsuccessful in securing enough supplies for themselves, much less for the entire Division. While in Manchester one drunken soldier in DeCourcey's Brigade shot and murdered a fellow soldier at 2:00 p.m. on Friday, September 18, 1962. Apparently, General Morgan went ahead to Manchester ahead of the column because Dr. Benjamin Stevenson reported that "Gen. Morgan came up a couple of hours later and immediately ordered a Court Martial trial of said soldier."[39]

One would think it odd that General Morgan would order a court martial while being pursued by Confederate cavalry. But, Morgan was an attorney before the war. He knew that his troops would have to have disciple to the highest degree to survive the upcoming ordeal. Furthermore, Morgan knew that bringing justice to the guilty party would set the correct example to maintain order and disciple among his troops. Dr. B. F. Stevenson of the 22nd Kentucky Infantry Regiment reported in his diary that "Saturday 19th, Court Martial tried, convicted, and sentenced prisoner to death." The next day Dr. Stevenson's diary simply read, "20th, sentence executed."[40] The 7th Division troops got the idea. They were in a desperate situation and everyone had to carry out his duty or suffer the consequences. Morgan's insistence upon procedural due process through a trial simply reflected his legal training. Executing the guilty soldier reflected his military bent toward instant obedience and discipline among the troops.

One of the companies of the 22nd Kentucky Infantry was organized in or close to Clay County, Kentucky. On September 18, 1862, two of the wives of soldiers belonging to the 22nd Kentucky Infantry came to Manchester to visit their respective husbands. One of the wives was pregnant. Shortly after the main column arrived, she began to experience birth pains. The baby was on the way! Dr. Stevenson reported that he was called upon to deliver the baby. Dr. Stevenson later reflected in a letter to his wife that,

A baby –'Picture it, think of it, dissolute man!' – a live 'gal' baby born in the midst of ten thousand soldiers and never a fig leaf in sight to cover its nakedness.

'The muckle black deil fly away wi' the brat.'

I was compelled to tear up two of my shirts to make swaddling bands And slips in which to dress it. Tis some comfort, however, to know That I had taken most of the wear out of them. Can't you replace them Soon? Life and death you see march with equal step all along the Pathway of life from the cradle to the grave.[41]

With his troops rested and reorganized for a long, arduous march to the Ohio River, Morgan ordered a hundred wagons burned on Sunday evening, September 21, 1862, around 10 p.m. Dr. B. F. Stevenson summed up the situation when he stated, "Stripping for a fight or a foot race, whichsoever may befall us, we are in trim for what may come." [42]

Morgan sent a Captain Adams ahead, probably on Sunday morning, September 21, 1862, on the road to Booneville and Proctor to locate supplies.[43] Captain Adams was a supply officer who Morgan praised as "faithful and energetic." [44] Once again Morgan displayed good leadership characteristics by praising his officers and men.

Chapter 11
Confederate Pursuit

Morgan's Federal troops arrived at Manchester on Saturday, September 20, 1862. As they arrived, elements of Stevenson's 8,000 Confederate troops were "close on their heels" capturing any stragglers who were unable to keep up with the Federal column.[1] Somewhere around Manchester, Stevenson received a message from General Kirby Smith to withdraw his force. Smith ordered Stevenson to join forces with General Bragg at Harrodsburg. On September 25, 1862, Lieutenant-Colonel (C.S.A.) George William Brent sent a dispatch to Col. (C.S.A.) George G. Garner advising him that Brigadier-General Stevenson had been ordered to Harrodsburg.[2] (One infers from the dispatch that Stevenson was ordered to Harrodsburg prior to September 25, 1862.)

On September 22, 1862, Major General John P. McCown (C.S.A.) reported back to Knoxville that General Morgan had abandoned Cumberland Gap on September 17, 1862. McCown reported in this dispatch that Stevenson's supply train, towards the rear of the advancing Confederate column, did not move from Cumberland Gap until September 20, 1862.[3] From these dispatches it can be inferred that some time between September 22 and September 25, General Stevenson turned away from pursuing Morgan and headed for

Harrodsburg.

Morgan reported that elements of John Hunt Morgan's cavalry skirmished with the Federal column on the road to Proctor. Paul Grogger of the 2nd Tennessee, U.S.A., stated in his memoirs that he arrived in Proctor on Monday, September 22, 1862.[4] Elements of John Hunt Morgan's cavalry were on reconnaissance missions keeping John Morgan apprised of George Morgan's movements. Hence, Stevenson probably broke off his pursuit on September 22, 1862, and John Hunt Morgan began his pursuit the same day.

General Smith ordered John Morgan into eastern Kentucky on September 19, 1862. Morgan proceeded to Richmond, Kentucky and arrived there on September 20, 1862. John Morgan then headed towards Irvine, Kentucky, the following day. Morgan sent out reconnaissance units to find the Federal column after arriving at Irving. These were the Confederate elements referred to by Paul Grogger who they encountered on the road to Proctor, Kentucky. John Morgan learned that the Federal column was headed towards Proctor, most likely from captured stragglers and George Morgan's bogus message intercepted by the Confederates indicating that the Federal column was headed for Maysville.

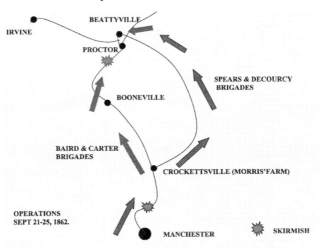

Evacuation by George Morgan and 7th Division
from Manchester to Beattyville, Ky.

John Morgan realized that Proctor was a tactical objective of the Federal column for two reasons. First, Proctor had a "large steampowered flour mill, a potential source of Yankee bread."[5] This would give the Federals an opportunity to make not only bread, but hardtack as well. Hardtack was a flour and water biscuit. It was three and one-eighth by two and seven-eights inches in length and width, and nearly half an inch thick. One day's ration was usually nine or ten per man. Since the Federals had to abandon Cumberland Gap because of a lack of food, capturing Proctor and its flour mill would have been a welcomed asset.[6] Second, Proctor was on the Kentucky River and on the way to Maysville via Booneville and Mt. Sterling.[7]

John Morgan ordered his approximately 900 cavalrymen to dash to Proctor as soon as possible. They arrived before the Federal troops on the night of September 22, 1862, and burned the flourmill, denying George Morgan's troops the food they desperately needed.[8] John Morgan then withdrew his cavalry to wait for another opportunity to delay the Federal column.

John Hunt Morgan understood his role in this operation to delay the column until Stevenson could move up from George Morgan's rear and destroy the Federal 7th Division. John Morgan also understood General Humphrey Marshall's role to intercept George Morgan at Mt. Sterling, or strike him in his flank.[9] However, John Morgan didn't know that Stevenson had been ordered to Harrodsburg on or about September 22, 1862. Thus, there was no Confederate pursuit from George Morgan's rear. Marshall never moved from Mt. Sterling because of the Confederate uncertainty as to George Morgan's intentions. Nevertheless, John Morgan thought Marshall was either coming down the Pound Gap-Mount Sterling Road to intercept the Federal column, or he would intercept him at West Liberty. Neither belief was true. Inefficient battlefield communications of the day no doubt contributed to John Morgan's misunderstanding. All John Morgan knew was that he was on his own to stop the advance of 10,000 Federal troops, while he had only approximately 900 cavalry to do the job in terrain unsuitable for cavalry operations. If Kirby Smith expected John Morgan to destroy the 7th Division, General John Hunt Morgan was on an impossible mission.

Chapter 12
Painful March to Hazel Green

Late on Sunday evening, September 21, 1862, or very early Monday morning, September 22, 1862, the Federal column left Manchester and headed towards Proctor. Early Monday a driver drove a caisson "too near the side of a difficult turn in the road."[1] Caissons are mule-drawn, two-wheeled wagons used to pull artillery ammunition. The driver made a turn too close to the edge of a hill and the caisson overturned. The driver sustained a bruised body and a broken arm, but thankfully the ammunition failed to detonate. This particular caisson contained percussion shells. Percussion shells detonate upon impact, which means that a jolt, such as a caisson turning over, could have caused the shells to explode. The Federal troops were thankful that no explosion occurred and then tried to upright the caisson. The teamsters tried to take the mules out of their harness before turning the caisson upright. During this process, a shell shifted, causing an explosion that resulted in a dozen or more secondary explosions. An imbedded reporter with the *Cincinnati Gazette* described the scene as follows:

And such an explosion! And such destructive and hair-bread escape! Coming up soon after I gazed on the scene with astonishment. All the spokes were cut clean from the rim of the wheel as though by a dull axe in a giant hand. Rifles lying on or fastened to the caisson were left but a blackened and beat on tube. A mule's leg was cut square off as though by the hand of a surgeon; and yet not a man killed! Two were seriously harmed and wounded, but not fatally, and how as many escaped was little short of a miracle. [2]

The explosion created such a noise that Morgan expected a Confederate attack for some time.

The road to Proctor diverged at a farmhouse owned by the Morris family. At this farmhouse Morgan divided his command sending Baird's and Carter's brigades to Proctor via Booneville. He sent Spears and De Courcy's brigades directly to Proctor. The Federal column encountered skirmishes along the way from elements of John Hunt Morgan's Confederate cavalry.[3]

The Federal column reached Proctor on Tuesday, September 23, 1862, only to find that the night before the Confederate troops, under John Hunt Morgan, had burned the flourmill. This was a devastating blow to the hungry Union troops. George W. Morgan's troops did manage to surprise some of John Morgan's cavalry who were still lingering around Proctor. The Union troops managed to almost surround the Confederates, but upon realizing their situation, the rebels made a hasty withdrawal.[4]

Arriving in Proctor, the hungry Union soldiers began their usual hunt for food. At a house known as the "Mountain House", several Kentucky Union soldiers entered the kitchen. One soldier placed his hand over the muzzle of his Belgian gun. He then began to play with the lock of the musket with the toe of his shoe. Unfortunately, the gun was loaded and a cap had been installed. A cap was a small explosive device placed on the gun, which when struck by the hammer, ignited the gunpowder. In other words, the gun was loaded and cocked. The soldier's gun discharged and he lost a finger and part of another and also wounded both hands. "The ball cut the tip of his ear and passed through the rim of his hat." [5] Despite the pleadings and admonitions of their sergeants, another soldier discharged his gun in a similar fashion resulting in rubbing "the skin off his nose."[6] The carelessness exhibited in these incidents indicated more than just inattention to detail. The men were beginning to become fatigued.

The grim business of withdrawing 10,000 troops over rugged terrain amid the constant harassment of John Hunt Morgan's cavalry began to take its toll on men and material. Owen Johnston Hopkins of the 42nd Regiment of the Ohio Infantry Volunteers, stated, "I lost the sole from my right boot a few days after leaving Manchester, and marching up and down the foothills of the Cumberland Mountains, over the rocky roads and thorny paths of the skirmish line, I suffered terribly, — but in this I was not alone. Hardly a man was fit to be seen for want of clothing." [7]

Lack of water also became a very serious threat to the troops. The drought of 1862 became one of the driest on record. The only water sources available to the Union troops were a "few springs and stagnating, scum-covered pools in the deepest recesses of otherwise dusty riverbeds."[8] Water would accumulate in crevices in cliffs along the way sometimes 80 to 100 feet deep. The soldiers would pull the only water available out of these cliffs.[9] One day they marched 34 miles before they found water. "So constantly and dreadfully did we suffer for want of it, that we began to talk of the distant Ohio as the end of all human desires. At another time, we were without water for about fifty hours. Our tongues were parched with thirst, and when at length water was obtained in the horse tracks on a low, flat piece of ground, it was fought for by us like so many wolves." [10]

Hunger was another major problem for the Union troops. They would steal an occasional pig or chicken when the opportunity arose. Every time the Federal troops passed a cornfield, troops would help themselves to the corn. Obviously, the Kentuckians who lived along the escape route did not appreciate hungry Federal troops stealing their corn. The troops rationalized that the Kentuckians owed them the corn since they were fighting for the Country.

After "liberating" some corn for the Union cause, the Union troops would take their bayonets and punch holes in a tin cup. They used the tin cup as a grater, grating the corn to make a course corn meal. Private Owen Johnston Hopkins reported in his diary that:

Our tin plates were converted into 'graters,' by means of which we reduced the hard corn to a course meal, and this, boiled to a 'mush'; or else the corn was simply parched, serving as food in this way for the half-famished soldiers. A small slice of bread or a cracker — before either entirely disappeared — commanded fabulous prices; ten dollars offered, with more buyers than sellers. We frequently went 48 hours without a morsel of anything. Staring famine elicited no murmuring, no complaint.[11]

"To grit corn along the march the men curved a tin plate over a smooth pole or rail and punched it full of holes with a bayonet. Sometimes they used a piece of old stovepipe, or a sheet of tin nailed over a board. Almost every individual, squad or group was equipped with such a miniature mill."[12]

Federal troops obtained pumpkins along the route and baked them. Food was so scarce that the hungry soldiers ate acorns, nuts, and any other edible plant or root they could find. Often times one group of soldiers used the still burning campfire of a preceding group to cook what they gathered on the route.[13] On one occasion several soldiers passed a farmhouse with a stand of thirty beehives. They were so hungry that they raided the hives and devoured the honey, but not before being stung by the angry bees.[14]

The Federal column brought with them over a hundred head of cattle from Cumberland Gap. The men enjoyed fresh beef the first few days of the march. However, the Federal army was usually in such a hurry, that they did not have time to slaughter and roast fresh beef at their leisure.

General Morgan knew how important it was to respect Kentuckians' private property. Therefore, he issued an order that no livestock found during the march could be killed and eaten without paying for it. On one occasion, a soldier aimed his gun at a "razorback" or "elm peeler", otherwise known as a mountain hog. About that time General Carter rode by and noticed the soldier drawing a bead on the hog. The soldier expected to be reprimanded by the general. Instead, with a twinkle in his eye, General Carter said, "Don't kill anything for waste." The soldier understood the hidden message and waited until the general was out of sight before he killed the hog.[15]

The officers suffered from hunger along with the enlisted men. One day General Morgan had only an ear of parched corn to eat. "Another day his entire staff had only twelve potatoes."[16] Ten women, including wives and daughters of some of the officers, traveled with the army to be near their husbands and fathers. Only officers were afforded this privilege. One day General Morgan rode along the column when he came upon the wife of one of his colonels. She looked rather pale and faint. He stopped and asked, "I hope you are not ill." "Oh, no," she replied, "I am well, General." Then she added, "I have eaten but once in forty-eight hours."[17] No one was immune from the hardships of this fabled march to the Ohio.

On Wednesday, September 24, 1862, the troops started marching for Hazel Green. During this march, once again, the soldiers created a self-inflicted disaster. One careless soldier threw down a loaded gun on a stack of loaded guns. One or two of the guns discharged as they hit the ground killing two soldiers.[18] Finally, on Thursday, September 25, 1862 the Federals reached Hazel Green. Except for an occasional skirmish, the march to Hazel Green was relatively uneventful. George Morgan rested his command for only one day before departing.

After withdrawing from Proctor, General John H. Morgan realized that the Federal column would have to go through Hazel Green because it was on the Pound Gap-Mt. Sterling Road. John Morgan figured that the Federals would turn west at Hazel Green and then head towards Mt. Sterling, ultimately making their way for Maysville. With this in mind, John Morgan ordered his men to ride towards Hazel Green as fast as possible to intercept George Morgan and the 7th Division. Fortunately for the Federals, George Morgan and his troops arrived at Hazel Green ahead of the Confederate cavalrymen.[19] John Morgan lost his opportunity to strike the Federal column at Hazel Green, but, more importantly, he then realized that George Morgan and the 7th Division were not headed for Maysville via Hazel Green. Instead, the Federals continued to march towards West Liberty. Even from West Liberty, however, the Federal column could still turn west and head towards Maysville.

John Morgan reviewed his map and realized that he must slow down the Union column somewhere between Hazel Green and West Liberty until help could arrive from Humphrey Marshall.

John Hunt Morgan's cavalrymen riding to intercept the Union column under command of George Washington Morgan. Re-enactment photograph taken by Lewis D. Nicholls.

Chapter 13
The Road to West Liberty

The Federal army left Hazel Green on Friday, September 26, 1862, and moved towards West Liberty, four abreast like a long serpent several miles long. A small unit of John Morgan's cavalry watched the Federal front, rear, and flanks, monitoring for a weakness they could exploit.[1] A Confederate attack would not be long in coming.

Rumors ran rapidly through the 7th Division. As lead columns crossed the Mt. Sterling-Pound Gap Road, two local pro-Union families told George Morgan that a large Confederate force of several thousand was preparing an attack to his front.[2] The rumor spread quickly from the front to the rear of the column. Every soldier braced for the anticipated attack from the front.

Suddenly, screaming rebels attacked the middle of the column with two companies of dismounted cavalry under the command of Captain Will Jones. John H. Morgan, his staff, and Major Breckinridge rode ahead to watch the action; however, operational command of the attack belonged to Jones. Jones attacked the rear guard of De Courcy's brigade, the second brigade from the front of the column. Captain Jones' Confederate forces struck with such fury that they killed and wounded several soldiers and captured twelve prisoners.[3]

The location of the attack was a surprise to the Union troops who suspected it would come on the front of the column.

Union Quartermaster Stubbs shouted to the front that an attack had occurred. George Morgan ordered two to three regiments to the rear to engage the ambushers. However, by the time these Union regiments arrived at the point of attack, the Confederates had already disappeared into the forested countryside.

Morgan's cavalry hid in the woods on many occasions before dismounting to ambush the Federal column. A cavalry charge is a romantic depiction of making war, but it usually got a lot of men wounded or killed. John Hunt Morgan's favorite tactic was for his men to dismount to ambush unsuspecting Federal troops. Re-enactment photograph taken by Lewis D. Nicholls.

Two companies of the 22nd Kentucky Infantry guarded approximately one hundred cattle traveling with the column. They were behind the ambushed column. In an effort to assist the ambushed Union soldiers, two companies of the 22nd pushed rapidly forward, leaving the cattle unguarded except for several cattle drivers. The dismounted Confederate cavalry seized this opportunity to launch a second attack on the unprotected herd and cattle drivers. They killed two of the cattle drivers and scattered the entire herd.[4] By the time the Federal soldiers could react, the Confederates were, once again, dissolved into the wooded countryside. The attack left casualties on both sides. The Federal soldiers killed six Confederate horses and their riders.[5] The Federals did manage to round up some, but not all, of the scattered cattle.

The Confederate attacks were a partial success. John Morgan ordered the attack hoping it would slow down the column until Marshall's troops arrived. After the attack, George Morgan's troops made camp a few miles from the ambush site, employing a skirmish line for security. The attack failed because it did not create the confusion that falls upon an undisciplined military unit. An imbedded reporter with the 7th Division reported in the *Cincinnati Gazette*, "There was, however, no confusion or anxiety manifest except for something to eat."[6] Attacks such as these were bound to leave the Union soldiers apprehensive and feeling vulnerable to an imminent attack around every bend on the trail. Despite the uncertainty of this ambush, the disciplined Union troops effectively dealt with the threat in a professional manner. George Morgan had adequately trained these men for battle.

A battle is a fluid encounter requiring battlefield commanders to adjust to the ever-evolving battlefield situation. George Morgan was a very security minded commander. He adhered to the principle of security, saving the lives of many of his soldiers. George Morgan moved his Union column as quickly as possible to stay out of harm's way. But now, John Hunt Morgan's Confederate cavalry found the Union column, and security was George Morgan's main issue. The "hit and run" tactics of the Confederate cavalry required that Morgan adjust to the changing battlefield situation by placing pickets on his left and right flanks. However, this type of tactical adjustment by the Union column carried its own set of problems.

Most of the roads were nothing more than dirt trails along a valley of steep hills on each side of the road. Vast forests lined either side of the road with thickets that would cut a man's clothes and flesh to shreds. A picket traveling through thorny thickets parallel to the road would have a difficult time trying to keep up with the moving column. Morgan now realized that the time had come for him to order pickets along his flanks, despite the fact that it would significantly slow down the column. With John Morgan's Raiders firing shots at the Union column all along the road behind trees and rocks, security now took precedence over speed.

On Friday morning, September 27, 1862, the 7th Division moved along the road through a small ravine. Morgan moved "with great caution. Skirmishers lined the hill sides, and every man was at his post."[7] Future progress was going to be deliberate and slow. Every time they approached a crossroad, Federal units would proceed along the crossroad, establishing roadblocks to prevent a surprise attack. The Federal troops would cross the road in safety. Once they were across the road, the flanking roadblocks would withdraw and catch up with the rest of the column. This process would be repeated again and again.[8]

It was during one of these maneuvers that the lead element of the Federal column came upon a large body of the enemy's cavalry.[9] The Rebel unit was actually General John Hunt Morgan, Major Breckinridge, and a subordinate commander by the name of Alston and several others. The Rebels had ridden to a creek where they dismounted and were watering their horses.[10] Major Kershner of the 16th Ohio Regiment stumbled upon them and ordered a skirmish line. The Union soldiers managed to fire eight to ten shots at the Rebels.[11] The hill was too steep and provided cover, resulting in the Union soldiers overshooting the Rebels. An unnamed Confederate soldier who was present described what happened next. "Death or capture seemed inevitable. But with perfect coolness Morgan shouted, 'Tell Colonel Breckinridge to advance; Major Jones, open your guns.' The regiment fell back over the hill, and we in greater hurry evacuated those premises."[12] Major Kershner ordered artillery to come forward. The artillery arrived within only a few minutes. But, it was too late! The Rebels had made their escape.[13] Neither side sustained any casualties, but the Federals lost "a fine mule, with a case of surgical instruments, saber and canteen was captured, and two horses lay dead, shot by rifle balls."[14]

Later, after withdrawing, John Hunt Morgan noticed some local civilians approaching him. The quick-witted John Morgan told Alston to tell the approaching civilians that Morgan was the Union Colonel DeCourcey. The Confederate officers would initially deceive the civilians until the Confederates could figure out whose side they supported. When the civilians rode into speaking distance Alston said, "That's Colonel DeCourcey. Why, the boys told us DeCourcey's brigade was behind, and we were mighty glad to see you." [15] At this moment a rare rain started to fall, requiring the Confederate officers to don their gum cloths or raincoats. The raincoats covered the officers' gray Confederate uniforms. Posing as the Union Colonel DeCourcey, John Hunt Morgan asked, "Wouldn't you like to join us?" "Oh, no," replied the civilian. "We can do you more good at home, killing the d____d secesh." Secesh was a Union Civil War term meaning Southerners who supported secession from the Union. Northerners applied it with a derogatory connotation. Morgan then said with a sweet approving smile, "Oh, have you killed many secesh?" One of the civilians replied, "I reckon we have. You'd laughed if you had seen us make Bill (a Kentucky Union supporter) kill his brother." "What did you do it for?" asked Morgan. The civilian replied, "Why you see Bill went South, and we burned his house, and he deserted; we arrested him, and said we were going to hang him as a spy: he said he'd do any thing if we let him off, that his family would starve if we hung him. Last Wednesday we took him, and made him kill his brother Jack. He didn't want to do it, but we told him we'd kill them both if he didn't, and we made him do it." [16]

Morgan kept a straight face throughout the civilian's demented description of how they committed murder. Morgan pumped him for all the information he could on the Union column's movements. They gave Morgan information on George Morgan's strength, the politics of citizens ahead, and of the conditions of the road ahead.[17] Morgan finally revealed his true identity after he satisfied himself that no more information could be garnered from these rascals. Morgan told them that he would hang them, but he failed to carry through with the threat. As one soldier stated who witnessed the event, "Unfortunately, however, General Morgan's leniency, which always got the better of him when he paused to think, induced him to spare them."[18]

At this point Gen. George Morgan believed that a strong force of Confederates under the command of General Humphrey Marshall had come down from Mt. Sterling and occupied West Liberty.[19] George Morgan approached West Liberty cautiously. All the way the Confederates continued to snipe at the Union column. George Morgan's scouts reported that there were no Confederate troops in West Liberty. Lead elements of the Union column entered West Liberty on Saturday, September 27, 1862.[20] The remainder of the Union column entered West Liberty on Sunday morning the 28th. The imbedded unnamed reporter with the *Cincinnati Gazette* described West Liberty as follows:

By the dawn of the Lord's Day we saw a wretched looking, dilapidated county seat. Half the houses without inhabitants; nearly all of them with broken windows and a woe begone aspect. Ten days previously Humphrey Marshall had passed through toward Mt. Sterling, with a brigade of rebels. Between rebel marauders and starving Federal soldiers, the country in the immediate vicinity was, comparatively, stripped of everything eatable. The army remained at West Liberty long enough to kill twenty

*head of cattle, and for each man to get a slice of beef, and still farther to
lighten knapsacks and wagons, that nothing not absolutely necessary should
impede our onward progress.[21]*

George Morgan rested for two days in West Liberty.[22] Paul
Grogger of the 2nd Tennessee Federal Army remembered his stay in
West Liberty as follows:

*We camped in a small river bottom. We killed a good many hogs
while we stayed there and helped ourselves, for our provisions was already
a getting very short and we was obliged to be a little shifty. What little meat
we had taken along from the Gap was already consumed, and our crackers
(hardtack) was not far behind.*

*At the start we lived a good deal on corn ears, but they soon got too
hard and we commenced gritten the corn and made us a little mush in our
tin cups every time we stopped. Sometimes we would carry our corn all day
before we would get the chance to make meal out of it, or risk of getting any
more.*

*At West Liberty, before we started again, we was also ordered to burn
our clothing and knapsacks that we had along, except one blanket. Consequently we had but one suit of clothes left, that what we had on our backs.[23]*

Killing hogs and making mush were not the only pastimes
George Morgan's troops enjoyed. Troops on both sides decorated the
courthouses as they entered the county seats of each county with
names, mottoes, and caricatures of Abe Lincoln and Jeff Davis. Sometimes some creative soldier wrote poetry on the walls of a courthouse.
While in West Liberty a reporter for the *Cincinnati Gazette* wrote that
one such poem in the courthouse was worth preserving. It read, "This
is the winter of our discontent made glorious summer by the advent

of that son of a b_____ from the Wabash."[24] The Gazette reporter indicated that he could not determine whether Union or Confederate soldiers made the derogatory comments. However, it probably was made about Abe Lincoln since Confederate forces had traveled through West Liberty about ten hours earlier on their way to Mt. Sterling.

While the lead elements of the Union forces were entering West Liberty on September 27, 1862, John Morgan's cavalry skirmished with them, capturing a few prisoners. "On the 28th, through the treachery of a guide, we (rebel forces) were led into an ambush, out of which we extricated ourselves with small loss."[25]

While occupying West Liberty, George Morgan sent out scouts and spies in every direction to gather as much intelligence as possible on John H. Morgan's position and movements.[26] George Morgan could not understand why the Confederate troops, under Humphrey Marshall, failed to intercept him at West Liberty. John Hunt Morgan desperately wanted an answer to this question as well. John Morgan knew that slowing down the Federal column, allowing Marshall to interrupt them, was the only chance he now had before the 7th Division slipped through his fingers.

Brigadier General Richard Montgomery Gano, Morgan's trusted subordinate commander, sent runners to General Marshall several times desperately requesting that Marshall converge on the Federal column. The only reply Morgan ever received from Marshall was, "Check the enemy all you can until I get there."[27] Basil Duke reported in his book the History of Morgan's Cavalry that, "Couriers had been constantly sent to both [Marshall and Stephenson], and to General Smith."[28] Basil Duke did not participate in the mountain campaign. He relied on a report from an unnamed soldier that rode with John Hunt Morgan in his quest to stop George Morgan. Nevertheless, the paramount question asked by both Morgans was, "Where is Humphrey Marshall?"

Chapter 14
Where is Humphrey Marshall?

General Smith expected George Morgan to head for Maysville once he left Cumberland Gap. Smith expected the Federal column to turn northeast at either Hazel Green or West Liberty to make their dash for Maysville.[1] On September 22, 1862, Major-General Kirby Smith sent a message to Brig. Gen. Humphrey Marshall in which he stated, "Until further notice you will remain at Mount Sterling, concentrating your forces at that point as rapidly as possible and holding them in readiness to move them at a moment's notice."[2]

On September 23, 1862, Kirby Smith sent a dispatch to Braxton Bragg advising him he was sending a force to Frankfort on September 24, 1862. He also stated that he was leaving Humphrey Marshall who "should be today at Mount Sterling, to watch and keep in check the enemy toward Covington. There is no indication of any force from Cumberland Gap nearer than Manchester."[3] On the same day, Kirby Smith sent a message to Humphrey Marshall ordering him to report his position and troop strength. Then, Smith ordered Marshall to proceed to "Paris to watch the enemy toward Covington."[4] Paris was to the west of Mt. Sterling, but sending Marshall to Paris made perfect sense if Smith were trying to use Marshall to screen Braxton Bragg from an army coming down from Cincinnati. Actually, Buell and the

Army of the Ohio started moving out of Louisville. At some point after September 23, 1862, Smith realized that there was no threat from Cincinnati. So, Smith ordered Marshall back to Mt. Sterling.

On September 24, 1862, General Kirby Smith sent a dispatch to General Marshall advising him that a prisoner had been taken at Proctor who said the Federal column was headed towards Maysville.[5] It is likely that the security minded George Morgan would have told his rank and file that they were headed for Maysville. This would have been consistent with the bogus information he had sent ahead with a young officer with the forged message to procure food near Maysville. It certainly appeared to General Smith that Maysville was the intended destination of the Federal column. Kirby Smith believed that George Smith was headed towards Mt. Sterling in order to reach Maysville.

On September 25, 1862, Kirby Smith sent a message to Humphrey Marshall stating that he believed that George Morgan would have to abandon his artillery and head towards Mt. Sterling from Proctor. Kirby Smith also ordered Generals Heth, Churchill, and Leadbetter to proceed to Mt. Sterling.[6] Smith stated in the dispatch that he believed that the four generals would converge on Mt. Sterling during the evening or late night of September 25, 1862. Smith was, of course, massing his troops believing that George Morgan and the Union 7th Division would emerge from the Kentucky mountains at Mt. Sterling. The Confederate plan to converge four Confederate units at Mt. Sterling, as the anvil, was coming together. On Thursday, September 25, 1862, George Morgan and the 7th Division arrived at Hazel Green. However, Smith thought the location of the Federal column was still consistent with his belief that George Morgan was headed towards Maysville via Mt. Sterling.

Edward O. Guerrant was a Kentuckian who served on Humphrey Marshall's staff during this time as a secretary and adjutant. Guerrant kept a very detailed diary that recorded the meeting between these four Confederate generals and Smith on Friday, September 26, 1862. Guerrant recorded that:

Five Generals at Head Quarters today, Smith, Heth, Churchill, Marshall, & Ledbetter. Four Brigades of Infantry now here at Mount Sterling. All under command of General E. Kirby Smith. General Smith is a tall, raw-boned, athletic man, very spare made, Cassius like; wears gold spectacles and full uniform. General Heth rather boyish in appearance, watery, pale gray eyes. Does not look like a General. Colonel Morgan and Captain Shawhan observing and harassing Federal Morgan near Hazel Green.[7]

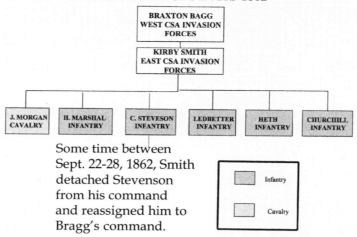

ORGANIZATION OF CONFEDERATE INVASION FORCES IN KY 1862

Some time between Sept. 22-28, 1862, Smith detached Stevenson from his command and reassigned him to Bragg's command.

Smith figured that if George Morgan were traveling towards Maysville, Owingsville would be the most likely town through which Morgan would have to progress. So, Smith ordered Marshall's command to go to Owingsville on Saturday, September 27, 1862. Guerrant recorded in his diary that their mission was to "cut off Morgan's retreat and capture him if possible."[8] Marshall was waiting at Owingsville, and three other Confederate generals were waiting at Mt. Sterling to intercept George Morgan and the Federal column. By Saturday, September 27, 1862, George Morgan proceeded cautiously toward West Liberty where he believed he would encounter a fight with Humphrey Marshall's army.

Guerrant recorded in his diary that on Sunday, September 28, 1862, Owingsville ladies entertained Marshall's soldiers. On Monday, September 29, 1862, Guerrant recorded, "No news from Colonel Morgan. A dispatch from General Smith about twelve M. ordered us back towards Lexington today, and at 12 p.m. we took up the line of march."[9]

It certainly seemed that Humphrey Marshall was cooperating with the unified command structure as he was previously ordered to do by Kirby Smith. Humphrey Marshall was not willfully disobedient, as feared by the Confederate high command. On the contrary, the evidence points to Marshall never receiving a message from Kirby Smith to proceed towards West Liberty to intercept George Morgan.

But, what about Gano's comments that he had sent several dispatches to Marshall for assistance, and Marshall responded with, "Check the enemy all you can until I get there."[10] Can Guerrant's statement of, " No news from Morgan," be reconciled with Gano's statement?

First, Marshall sent Captain John Shawhan and his cavalry to support John Morgan's cavalry. Shawhan was a fifty-two year old veteran of mountain warfare who served with Humphrey Marshall during the Mexican War. Marshall and Shawhan respected each other as evidenced by the fact that Shawhan joined Marshall when he was trying to raise an army. This could have been Marshall's way of supporting John H. Morgan during the operation against George Morgan and his Federal column. Guerrant stated in his diary when Union guerilla sympathizers killed Shawhan on Tygart Creek near present day Olive Hill, Kentucky, "O! War!! A brave soldier & honest man gone!!"[11] Apparently, Guerrant and others considered Shawhan a solid officer. For Marshall to send Shawhan indicates that Marshall was sincerely trying to assist John H. Morgan, within the discretion allotted him by General Smith.

If Marshall had an earnest desire to help John H. Morgan, why send only a small contingent of cavalry when Marshall had an army of over 3,000 at his command? The answer lies in the authority handed Marshall by General Kirby Smith. Smith and other Confederate leaders told Marshall to cooperate with the unified command structure during the Kentucky operation. This was in keeping with the principle of war of "unity of command." Marshall took his orders from General Kirby Smith, not from Colonel John H. Morgan. Marshall realized that any false move on his part, showing he was not a team player, would reflect adversely on him, especially considering that he had been warned to cooperate as late as September 21, 1862.[12] Therefore, Marshall could not afford to take off into the Kentucky mountains because a Colonel, not in his chain of command, sent a plea for help. All Marshall could do was send a message saying he would be there when he received an order from General Smith, who was in his chain of command.

If Marshall were awaiting a message from General Smith, why didn't he send a message to Smith advising him of the situation and the urgent plea for help from Morgan? Historians are unable to agree that Marshall sent such a message. There is just no record of a message ever being sent by Marshall to Smith. However, the Official Records of the Civil War occasionally make reference to messages being lost.

Even if Smith did receive a message from Marshall of John Morgan's plea for assistance, it is highly unlikely that Smith would order Marshall to charge into the mountains of eastern Kentucky to intercept George Morgan. As late as September 24, 1862, Smith believed that George Morgan was headed towards Mt. Sterling.[13]

To make matters worse for Marshall, he received confusing reports as to the 7th Division's actual location and destination. Parish Brickey was one of Marshall's soldiers. After the war he told his family that the 7th Division was headed for Richmond, Kentucky one day.

Thus, Marshall's troops would march toward Lexington. Then, the next day they would receive a report that the 7th Division was at West Liberty and headed for Mt. Sterling. So, they would reverse direction and march towards Mt. Sterling. Many of Marshall's troops were barefooted, starved, exhausted as they marched in response to each unconfirmed report of the 7th Division's location. All of these confused reports made it feasible for Marshall to stay in the Mt. Sterling-Owingsville area and wait to attack the 7th Division once it emerged from the eastern Kentucky wilderness.[14]

Smith and Marshall both still believed that George Morgan was headed for Mt. Sterling or Owingsville. On September 29, 1862, the Federal column left West Liberty and headed for the Ohio River somewhere between Portsmouth, Ohio, and the confluence of the Big Sandy River and the Ohio River at Catlettsburg, Kentucky. By the time Marshall realized that the 7th Division was headed for the Ohio River through eastern Kentucky, it was too late to intercept them.

Smith only needed to prevent George Morgan and his 10,000 Union troops from being a factor during the Confederate invasion of Kentucky. Smith was very concerned about Union General Don Carlos Buell coming down from Louisville with his 35,000 troops. However, Buell had only one thing on his mind — find Bragg and Smith and destroy them.[15] Buell did eventually find Bragg and Smith at the battle of Perryville, but that battle did not occur until October 8, 1862. Smith was content to keep 10,000 Union troops from massing with the rest of Buell's 35,000 troops. The most economic way Smith could accomplish this, the better.

"Economy of force" is another principle of war. "Economy of force" simply means to use only the minimum amount of force necessary to accomplish the mission. Smith, so far, was able to use only 900 cavalrymen to keep a force almost eleven times his size from influencing any action in the upcoming clash with Buell. This was a solid application of the "economy of force" principle of war. In other words, Smith had no reason to order Marshall into the mountains of eastern Kentucky as long as George Morgan was staying in eastern Kentucky. Smith indicated this line of thought in a letter to Humphrey Marshall on September 24, 1862, when Smith stated, "Should General Morgan turnoff at Proctor and make for Salyersville and Louisa, he should be pushed by the cavalry, and General Loring, on the Kanawha, notified by a trusty messenger of his line of retreat."[16] Being "pushed by the cavalry" meant pushing George Morgan away from Mt. Sterling and in an eastward direction towards Salyersville and Louisa.

Further evidence of this strategy was contained in Smith's dispatch to Bragg on September 24, 1862. Smith advised Bragg that, "Should he [George Morgan], after crossing the Kentucky, turn to the east and make for Salyersville and Louisa, I shall push him with the cavalry, and, leaving him to the ruin and demoralization that must overtake his army in that wild, mountainous country, will order all my disposable force to General Bragg's support."[17] Obviously, Smith thought that Morgan's 7th Division would perish in the wild mountains of eastern Kentucky. Smith figured that he would let the wild country of eastern Kentucky inflict mortal damage on the Union column and not risk any harm to his own troops. It appears that Smith never had any intention of sending Marshall into eastern Kentucky, so long as George Morgan kept moving away from central Kentucky where Buell and Smith would eventually collide at Perryville.

Marshall's statement, "Check the enemy all you can until I get there," reported by Gano, was Marshall's way of dealing with a subordinate commander's (Col. John H. Morgan) plea for help, especially when Marshall had no authority to take off into eastern Kentucky without the proper authorization from Gen. Smith.

By Monday, September 29, 1862, Smith figured that Morgan was headed for the mouth of the Big Sandy River.[18] Smith came to this realization after Morgan failed to turn left at West Liberty and head for Mt. Sterling. Therefore, Smith ordered Marshall back from Owingsville to Mt. Sterling. Smith knew it was too late for Marshall to intercept Morgan once he crossed West Liberty.[19]

To answer the question, "Where was Humphrey Marshall?" we can say that he was exactly where General Kirby Smith told him to be. Smith was not going to tell Marshall to engage George Morgan, unless Morgan made a move towards Owingsville or Mt. Sterling. Since George Morgan never made a move with the 7th Division toward central Kentucky, then Kirby Smith never ordered him to attack Morgan in eastern Kentucky!

Chapter 15
The Road to Grayson

On Monday morning, September 29, 1862, the Federal column headed out from West Liberty towards Grayson. Paul Grogger of the Federal 2nd Tennessee Regiment described the day as a " . . . pleasant autumn day and we felt a great deal revived from our days rest."[1] Not long into the march a shot rang out. One Union soldier fell to the ground. Union officers barked out orders inquiring if anybody saw from where the shot had come? Suddenly, a second shot added to the confusion as a second Union soldier fell to the ground. The Confederate sniper killed both of the Union soldiers. No Federal soldier saw from where the shots had come. Then, the muffled sound of ten thousand soldiers marching on dirt was all that could be heard once again.

The Confederate sniper was Tom Perry who rode with a company of Confederate cavalry commanded by Capt. John T. Williams.[2] Capt. Williams commanded Company C, 1st Regiment of the Kentucky Mountain Rifles, C.S.A., that had approximately 300 men.[3] While the Federal forces occupied West Liberty, several of them tore down a corn crib and stole all of the corn. Of course, the Union troops believed that they had only appropriated the corn to the Federal cause and saw nothing illegal about it. However, Tom Perry viewed it as just plain stealing since the corncrib belonged to him. He slipped out of his company and killed the first two unsuspecting Union soldiers that came into his gun sights. After killing the two soldiers, he rejoined his company.[4] The Union troops could tell that something was different about the Confederate pursuit after they left West Liberty.

George Morgan then received a report that the Confederates were headed to Grayson, fifty miles down the road. George Morgan realized that it was critical to arrive at Grayson ahead of John Hunt Morgan's cavalry. So, George Morgan issued the order for all of the troops "to burn all clothing blankets and other baggage that could be spared. Fires were kindled, and great numbers of overcoats and blankets were burned." The less nonessential equipment his men carried, the faster they could march.[5]

Near West Liberty, Confederate Capt. John T. Williams' company joined with John Morgan's cavalry. Williams' men were from Morgan County and thus, were thoroughly familiar with the terrain.[6] Armed with this knowledge, John Morgan gave John Williams command of the advance guard in an attempt to slow down the Federal column.[7] The Confederate attacks were now executed with more ferocity than before since Williams' cavalry knew where the best ambush sites existed.

The Federal troops marched towards Grayson and as the day wore on, it became very hot. Occasionally they crossed a hill that would sap their strength as they reached the top. They marched down into the hot valley and then followed the dried up creek bed of the Licking River. Since the creek bed had not seen water for over two months because of the drought, the route became extremely dusty. The reporter with the *Cincinnati Gazette* described the hot dusty march as follows: "These sands and these rocks and hills had drunk no water for near two months. Columns and clouds of dust—finer than the finest flour, rise at every foot-fall. It covers you—it fills your eyes and they burn and itch—you wipe and rub them and you add more dust. It fills your nose and mouth and throat—you thirst and get nothing but stagnant, tepid water; but on you tramp, tramp, tramp."[8]

Other Confederate attacks occurred at different points along the Federal column. Toward evening, the Federal First Tennessee Regiment came under an attack by Confederate ambushers. George Morgan dispersed his artillery pieces along the column so that he could apply artillery in a very short time at any point. As soon as the First Tennessee was attacked, George Morgan brought his closest artillery pieces to bear on the Confederate ambushers. The federal troops referred to these artillery pieces as "bullfrogs." The bullfrogs quickly dispersed the attacking Rebels.[9]

Some time on Tuesday, September 30, 1862, the Federal column reached the headwaters of the Little Sandy River located approximately 20 miles from Grayson.[10] The Federal column used the dry bed of the Little Sandy River as their road since it was the only means over which the artillery pieces could travel. A dirt road did exist adjacent to the river; however, often times the road became the dried up riverbed itself. But, there was another reason George Morgan ordered his column to use the dry riverbed as their road.

George Morgan and his staff most likely did not know exactly where they were because their maps were not very accurate. The imbedded reporter with the *Cincinnati Daily Gazette* stated, "Maps, however, are in great demand. Even a poor, mean thing called the war map, that gives you as vague an idea of our route as a Chinese map does of the countries of the barbarians! Every one is calculating the distance to the Ohio River. Shall we make it at Catlettsburg, Greenupsburg or Portsmouth? No one answers by authority, and on, on we marched."[11]

Although Morgan did not know his exact location, he knew to find a stream or creek and follow it downstream because the stream or creek would eventually take his column to a larger body of water. In this case, the larger body of water was the Ohio River. Catlettsburg is where the Big Sandy River empties into the Ohio River;

Greenupsburg is where the Little Sandy Rivers empties into the Ohio River; and Tygart Creek empties into the Ohio River on the Kentucky side near Portsmouth, Ohio. George Morgan was most likely following this principle knowing that he would eventually hit the Ohio River, but precisely where he would come out on the Ohio River, he was unsure. Once the column reached the headwaters of the Little Sandy River, Morgan and his staff had a better idea of where they were, and where they would finally come out at the Ohio River. The local residents told him that they were within 50 miles of the Ohio River. But, one elderly gentleman told Morgan, "out of 350 voters in this district, there are but thirty-three true Washington Union men."[12] Generally speaking, the eastern Kentuckians supported the Union. But, between West Liberty and Grayson, George Morgan and his Federal column encountered renewed and determined efforts by the local Confederate cavalry, lead by John T. Williams, and the local population to delay the Federal column.

The elderly gentleman who advised George Morgan of this hotbed of Confederate sympathy also told him, "My horses are hid in the woods to save them; two of my sons have been taken prisoners; but three others and my son-in-law are now ahead of you among your guides, and they know every wolf-path in these mountains."[13] During the conversation with Morgan, the elderly gentleman spied a young soldier in the Federal ranks whom he knew lived in the vicinity. The elderly gentleman saluted the young soldier and said to him, "James, they have robbed your father — your horse is gone — they have got nine horses from your family."[14] The War was now becoming personal for at least one Union soldier. The Country was unraveling at the seams. Soldiers on both sides knew that the struggle would have to be to the death. Either the Union or the Confederacy would have to perish. Both the Union and Confederacy could not co-exist.

George Morgan obtained additional intelligence from captured Confederate soldiers. During interrogation, the captured soldiers swore that they belonged to the advance guard of 14,000 soldiers under the commands of Generals Kirby Smith and General Humphrey Marshall.[15] The captured soldiers told the Federal officers that Generals Smith and Marshall were massing at Grayson to destroy the 7th Division.

Morgan's staff had two opinions about the intelligence these captured soldiers were feeding them. One group of Federal officers thought that the reports were credible. Why else would the Confederate cavalryman go to such extraordinary measures to slow the Federal advance? It must be to give the Rebels time to mass their troops in Grayson. The other school of thought was that the Federal column of 10,000 soldiers was just not that important. After all, George Morgan's troops were half starved and half naked, just barely strong enough to survive the march towards the Ohio River in retreat. George Morgan knew that there was another very large Federal force under the command of General Buell that the Rebels would have to destroy to keep Kentucky. Consequently, the only choice George Morgan had was to press on towards Grayson and give the Confederates a battle if they made a stand at Grayson.

George Morgan ordered his men to use the bed of the dried up Little Sandy River as the roadway towards Grayson. It was the only road large enough to accommodate the rolling artillery. As they entered the riverbed, the Federal troops noticed that, "high precipitous banks of sandstone" rose extremely high on both sides of the riverbed.[16] "Most of these cliffs were arching, and large trees growing over their extreme edges. In some places, for miles, you could see no crevice up which a body of men could scale them. Here we anticipated an ambush; for a few hundred men might stop the progress of ten thousand."[17] The Confederates wasted no time in putting together an ambush.

The Little Sandy riverbed twisted through a narrow system of gorges in Elliott County. One particular sharp bend was known as the Crackers Neck. Here, "the road rounded the base of a semicircular bluff."[18] John Morgan selected this site for an ambush. Company A, Breckinridge's battalion, and Company F, Duke's regiment, under the command of Major Breckinridge hid in the trees along the bank. George Morgan dispersed seventeen cavalrymen just in front of the Federal column. A Confederate soldier who participated in the ambush described what happened next.

"The [Federal] column came to within twenty yards of the line of ambush, and its head was nearly beyond the extreme flank of the two companies; in advance were seventeen cavalrymen, some sitting with their legs thrown over the pommels of the saddle, some eating pawpaws; the insignia of rank upon their shoulders could be easily distinguished. Suddenly over a hundred rifles belched forth death and fire — again their volley echoed through the mountains; when the smoke cleared away, the head of the column had disappeared like a wave broken upon a rock, and before a line could be formed or a gun unlimbered, we were gone, and laughed as we marched to the music of their guns shelling the innocent woods over the mountain from us."[19]

George Morgan sent the seventeen Union cavalrymen ahead to trigger just such an ambush. He no doubt calculated that seventeen cavalrymen were sufficiently large enough to defend themselves. However, under the cover of the concealed riverbank, an advance force of seventeen cavalrymen was just simply not large enough for self-protection. In response to this ambush, Morgan changed his tactics and placed a much larger force at the head of the retreating column and on his flanks. These larger forces were capable of conducting offensive operations against the marauding rebels and defend themselves from ambushes. Again, George Morgan adapted to the changing tactical situation applying the principles of security, economy of force, and mass to make the march safer for the troops. Morgan also employed the principle of offense by throwing stronger forces in front of and along the flanks of the column not only to defend the column but also to conduct offensive operations. These Federal offensive operations were so successful that George Morgan's troops drove the Rebels from their hot supper on three successive evenings.[20] The Rebels noted this change in tactics also. One Confederate soldier reported, "After this they [Federal troops] changed their tactics, and marched with a heavy line of skirmishers in front and upon both flanks."[21]

Crackers Neck located on Little Sandy River in Elliott County, Kentucky. Notice the sharp bend in the river with high cliffs on far side of the river. This is the location where seventeen Union cavalrymen were ambushed. Photograph taken by Lewis D. Nicholls.

Meanwhile, John Morgan and his troops labored under the illusion that General Humphrey Marshall was headed towards Grayson to destroy the 7th Division. John Morgan thought that Marshall would head off the Federal column at West Liberty also, but this too proved only to be a mirage. In truth, Marshall never got any closer than Mt. Sterling to the Federal column. Nevertheless, John Morgan thought that Marshall was coming to assist him. John Morgan figured that if he could delay long enough, Marshall would have the time he needed to move his troops into position near Grayson.

John Morgan's 900 cavalrymen and John T. Williams' 300 cavalrymen began a new tactic after the Crackers Neck ambush. They "fought vigorously with the ax and torch, felling trees, barricading the road, destroying bridges, and making every barricade cost a skirmish and time."[22] Judge John Frew Stewart was a young infantryman in the Union Fourteenth Kentucky Regiment who participated in the famed retreat. Judge Stewart recalled the retreat years later with this description. "During this entire memorable retreat, the enemy, probably a Division or more, harassed [George] Morgan's force on all sides, continually felling timbers in the roads before them and fighting in rear flanks and in front."[23] John Morgan certainly did not have a division of soldiers, but it must have seemed like it to John Frew Stewart and the beleaguered Federal column.

George Morgan countered the barricading of the dried road with large trees by calling on Captain William F. Patterson's engineers. The engineers cleared the blockades by removing trees and building bridges where needed to keep the column going.[24] George Morgan reported, "Frequent skirmishes took place, and it several times happened that while one Morgan was clearing out obstructions at the entrance of a defile, the other Morgan was blockading the exit."[25] During one instance, Patterson's engineers cut a road for four miles around obstructions too difficult to move.[26] The imbedded reporter with the *Cincinnati Commercial* newspaper reported, "We have had to dig new roads around burned bridges, cut out trees for miles, [and] . . . dig and dam for water."[27]

Finally, very late on Tuesday night, September 30, 1861, George Morgan ordered his column to halt for the night. The soldiers tried to rest. Soon many of the thirsty soldiers obtained their empty canteens and headed down the dried riverbed in search of some water to drink. They moved about a quarter of a mile down the riverbed when Confederate soldiers ambushed them. They scurried back to their camp and formed a skirmish line and the Union artillerymen fired a few volleys into the direction of the Rebels. The Confederates never followed them or offered any more resistance. Only one Union soldier, Captain Joseph D. Underdown, Co. K of the 2nd Tennessee, was slightly wounded. The exhausted Union troops then rested quietly and peaceably until the next morning, Wednesday, October 1, 1862.[28]

Morning began at 2:00 a.m. for the troops of the 42nd Ohio Infantry. The Confederates had obstructed the road at a deep, rocky gorge with huge rocks and fallen trees. Morgan sent several regiments forward to reconnoiter the road ahead. They found seven blockades obstructing their way. At a temporary road built around the burned bridge, the advanced party of the Federal column caught the Confederate troops busy obstructing the road. The Union troops attacked the Confederate troops and an artillery sergeant and a private of the 42nd captured two prisoners. One of the prisoners was a Confederate captain. The Union troops found two pieces of cornbread on the captured captain. The Union commander on the scene told the Federal private that as a prize for capturing the enemy soldiers, he could choose either the cornbread or the captured captain's saddle as a spoil of war. The private choose the cornbread. So hungry were the Federal troops in this late stage of the retreat that they even ate bitter acorns.[29]

On Wednesday morning at 4:00 a.m., the Federal column started towards Grayson despite the repeated attempts of the Confederate troops to stop, or at the very least slow down, their advance. The Confederate troops continued to blockade the road, but the Federal column was able to quickly clear it and move on. The Federal column occasionally sighted Confederate snipers, but they were quickly cleared and the Federals were able to march 22 miles before stopping at 2:00 a.m. on Thursday, October 2, 1862. The Federal troops were exhausted. They "slept soundly in the woods by [the] road side" only one mile from Grayson.[30]

Some time between Wednesday, October 1, and Thursday, October 2, 1862, George Morgan's soldiers came upon the Horton House built by Elijah Horton in 1838. Elijah Horton chose to build his house in the valley close to the banks of the Little Sandy River approximately ten miles from Grayson.[31] Many Carter County residents told stories for years of the two Morgan generals colliding in combat around the Horton house. It is difficult to separate fact from folklore, but considering the context in which the stories are told, and the actual historic events known to occur, a reasonable interpretation of the stories can be pieced together and woven into a probable accurate history.

John Hunt Morgan probably came upon the house as he proceeded ahead of the Union column looking for ambush sites. Mr. and Mrs. Horton, most likely Confederate sympathizers, invited the Confederate general for dinner. Mrs. Horton brought out her finest silverware and prepared a feast. General John Hunt Morgan dined royally until a neighbor galloped up on a horse to warn John Morgan that Union General George Morgan's advance parties were coming up the river.[32] John Morgan jumped on his horse and left the Horton house as quickly as possible. As the Union column advanced upon the Horton house, because they were hungry, the soldiers started stealing and killing the Horton's geese and chickens. One soldier, unable to swim, waded into the river chasing a goose and drowned. A Confederate sharpshooter, accompanying John Morgan, shot a second

Union soldier near the house as he attempted to mount his horse.[33] John Hunt Morgan and his small reconnaissance party rode back to his temporary headquarters located at the Mose Everman house just a mile or two northwest of Grayson currently owned by Mr. Clayton Burnett.[34]

The Horton house is located in Carter County, Kentucky where John Morgan likely had dinner. It has been moved from its original location down on the Little Sandy River. Photograph taken by Lewis D. Nicholls.

Several hours later, as General George Morgan approached Grayson, he took a small detachment of mounted soldiers from Lt. Col. Reuben Munday's Kentucky Battalion of cavalry during the night and reconnoitered Grayson. Morgan found out that there were no Confederate troops in Grayson as earlier reported by some of the local people. Consequently, he sent a messenger back to the main column ordering them to come on into Grayson.

Interestingly, around October 1, 1862, John H. Morgan received a message from Kirby Smith telling him to withdraw from the front of the Federal column. In the message Kirby told John Morgan "not to attempt further to impede his [George Morgan's] progress, but rather assist him to leave the State, and rejoin the main army at Lexington, or wherever it might be."[35]

The Union column entered Grayson all during the morning of Thursday, October 2, 1862 and completed the march into Grayson by early afternoon, Thursday, October 2, 1862. Thursday was a dry, hot, and dusty day. The Union troops were extremely thirsty and tired. As they entered Grayson, the reporter with the *Cincinnati Daily Gazette* reported the eerie sight. "Not an enemy was to be seen; not a single dog barked. The blockaders all scedaddled at 4 o'clock P. M. the day before."[36] The Cincinnati reporter continued to write, "Grayson makes a finer appearance than any town through which we have passed on the route. It has a respectable looking courthouse and schoolhouse and a finer looking church edifice than we have yet seen on all the road from the Gap; indeed, it is almost the only one seen within 200 miles worthy the name of a place of worship."[37]

George Morgan's troops marched through Grayson and camped in a "nice meadow" on the north side of town.[38] Today, this meadow is the campus of Kentucky Christian University. It was in this meadow that the Union troops grated their corn and baked cornbread cakes for the final push to Greenup. In this "nice meadow" they ate as much as they wanted.[39] The Union column rested until late afternoon when, once again, George Morgan gave the order to march at around 4:00 p.m. on Thursday, October 2, 1862. The Federal column started its final leg of the journey toward Greenupsburg. The Federal soldiers knew that they were only 25 miles from the Ohio River. Without a whimper the soldiers once again formed ranks and marched toward the grand Ohio River, where the tired and thirsty soldiers could quench their thirst, take a bath, and rest their tired, aching feet.

Four miles past Grayson, the road narrowed to a very narrow pass that the local people called "The Narrows." The road passed over a cliff overhanging the Little Sandy River. The road was just four inches wider than the wagon's width. By the time wagons of the 42nd Ohio Infantry came upon "The Narrows," it was dark. Nevertheless, the first two wagons safely negotiated the dangerous road. Unfortunately, the third, fourth, and fifth wagons fell over the cliff and into the Little Sandy River. Prudently, officers finally gave the order to halt the march until daylight.[40]

   They arrived in Oldtown, Kentucky, in Greenup County at midnight after a twelve-mile march.[41] They camped in Oldtown for a few hours until sunrise.

   The fact that no Confederate army was in Grayson waiting to pick a fight must have been a great relief to George Morgan and his staff. All of John H. Morgan's efforts to slow down the Federal column until Humphrey Marshall's soldiers could arrive from Mt. Sterling had been in vain. It was certainly a great disappointment to John Morgan. One of John Morgan's soldiers reflected later that :

The country was not fit for cavalry operations. The 30th passed away; the 1st Oct was half gone. From the morning of the 26th to noon of the1st, over five days, the Federals had marched not over thirty miles, less than six miles a day. We had done our work, but where was Marshall or Stephenson? Since the morning of the 29th we had been anxiously looking for news from them. Couriers had been constantly sent to both, and to General Smith. We knew that the enemy were living on meat alone, for we, in their front, went without bread for over three days, living on fresh beef, without salt, half-ripe corn, and the luscious pawpaws. If Marshall or Stephenson had attacked, the army of the gap would have been prisoners. Whoever was to blame, let him be censured. Morgan, with raw recruits, badly armed, accomplished his part of the task.[42]

Chapter 16
The Road to Greenup

On Friday, October 3, 1862, at Oldtown the Federal column once again arose at sunrise to an overcast morning. They began their march from Oldtown without breakfast. They stopped at 9:00 a.m. for only 30 minutes and made coffee.[1] The Federal column followed the road in which some places included the sandy shoreline of the Little Sandy River. As they proceeded closer to the Ohio River on their way towards Greenupsburg, some water began to appear in the riverbed. Along the shoreline, the sand was deep and hot, burning the feet of the many soldiers whose shoes literally had worn off their wearers' feet.[2]

Only a few miles north of Grayson stood the old Trilight Inn at the crossroads of the road leading to the small village of Pactolus. At the crossroads stood the home of Nannie Botts. The large armies marching close to her home intrigued Nannie, a small child at the time. Her parents were not intrigued because they knew that these soldiers were hungry. Hungry soldiers meant that they helped themselves to all of the family's chickens, hams, etc. So, Nannie's parents hid the hams and as many chickens as possible from the hungry soldiers. Nannie's parents told her to stay inside the house, but Nannie and her brother and sister, curious and unafraid, scampered out of the house and climbed upon the fence to watch the marching soldiers.

They first saw the remaining cattle pushing and shoving their way along the route. Next, a cavalry unit trotted along until they came to the house and saw the children. The officer in charge realized children meant parents, and parents meant a farmhouse had to be nearby. In a few minutes, the soldiers found the farmhouse and decided it was worth investigating for food. They "ransacked the house, found the hams, and as chickens ran squawking and crazily about the yard, they, too, were taken, speared with bayonets—and many a soldier rode on with a screaming, bleeding chicken on his bayonet, to be roasted later."[3]

During this encounter, one Union soldier was deeply moved by the sight of one of the little girls. She must have reminded him of his own child. The soldier reached into his pocket and pulled out a bright hair ribbon. He tied it around the little girl's pretty hair. The soldier then moved out with his unit. She treasured it for years until it was worn to shreds.[4]

The Union column continued to march forward for several more hours. Finally, the effect of the 170-mile march took its toll on both horses and men. Both were exhausted. Some of the men, in an effort to lighten their loads, threw heavy cannonballs, muskets, packs and other equipment into the Little Sandy River.[5] In the early 1900's the Eastern Kentucky Railroad was built close to this location. The engineers constructing the railroad changed the channel of the Little Sandy River leaving only a large pond. This pond is where the soldiers threw their equipment into the Little Sandy River. Today, this pond is known as the Anglin Pond, located on either side of Kentucky State Route 1, choked with lily pads and algae in the summer. Later owners of the property entertained themselves during the summer by looking for these artifacts on the bottom of the pond.[6]

Anglin pond where some of George Morgan's troops threw equipment into the Little Sandy River. Photograph taken by Lewis D. Nicholls.

Near Oldtown, the Federal column came upon a spring along their route. The spring was 36 inches deep and could replenish itself every two hours. The thirsty soldiers gathered around the spring and drank it dry. That same spring still exists today. It is located on property owned by Mr. Bill Claxon in Oldtown, Kentucky. Mr. Claxon uses it as his supply of water for his home.[7]

Past the spring, the road turned onto the narrow shelf along the sandy riverbank of the Little Sandy River. The riverbank was too narrow to accommodate passage of the field artillery and the sandy shoreline could not support the heavy artillery. Morgan called upon Patterson's engineers once again. They widened the shoreline and supported the sandy soil so that it would allow passage of the heavy field artillery. Naturally, this slowed down the progress of the column, but by midnight the column was once again moving at a brisk pace and making good time.[8] "The moon shone with a silvery brightness, and the air was unusually warm. Hunger, fatigue and sore feet compelled many to coil up under a bush or by the wayside before the bugle sounded for a halt."[9]

The arrow points to the small structure that covers the spring that the Federal troops drank dry as they passed through Oldtown, Greenup County, Kentucky. The spring is still in use as a private water source for the current owner. Photograph taken by Lewis D. Nicholls.

As the day wore on, the hot dry sand worked its way into the men's boots causing their feet to be scoured until they were raw and bleeding. Around 11 a.m. a hard rain began to fall.[10] The rain cooled the men with its refreshing wetness, but as soon as it stopped, the extremely high humidity caused the men to break out in another debilitating sweat that sapped what little strength they retained. Exhaustion overcame many of the men and they just collapsed where they stood. The reporter with the *Cincinnati Daily Gazette* described one such soldier. "Down he threw himself on the rough, hard ground, under an old pear tree standing out alone in a waste and barren field. The ground had been tramped and rolled by hoof and body of all domestic animals from time immemorial. There he lay and slept though the heavens gathered blackness and the rain fell—there he tried to find rest, though the ants crawled all over him and sought shelter from the rain in his clothes and even in his scanty hair, till a large proportion of the entire army had passed on before."[11]

As the rain fell, the dusty roads became extremely muddy. This condition made each step that much harder for the men to trudge forward. Men's muscles became tired and stiff. Finally, the men passed the word along the column that, "Only ten miles to the Ohio River!"[12]

Shortly after noon, advance elements of the 42nd Ohio Infantry "emerged from a rugged gorge into the valley of the Ohio River, and saw before it, half a mile away, the little town of Greenupsburg, its white walls and spires bright in the October sunshine. The people, as we approached, came out to welcome the lost Army of Cumberland Gap."[13] The advanced elements of the column emerged from the eastern Kentucky wilderness at the present day intersection of State Route 1 and US 23 at Greenup, Kentucky.

As additional elements emerged from the rugged gorge, the men saw the hills of the State of Ohio in the distance across the Ohio River. One officer on General Morgan's staff commented to the correspondent for the *Cincinnati Daily Gazette*, "There, Items, there is God's country!" The correspondent replied, "Yes, there is indeed God's country once more!"[14]

Soon, the first brigade in the column caught a glimpse of the Ohio River. "At the glad sight, a thrilling shout went up, and 'The Ohio! The Ohio!' rolled like thunder down the excited line. Each regiment and brigade took it upon turn till 'The Ohio! The Ohio!' rose and fell in prolonged and jubilant acclamation for miles away, along the weary column. It recalled the time when the German army sent up in a wild shout, 'The Rhine! The Rhine!' as they once more came in sight of their native stream, and joy and gladness filled every heart."[15] For most of the troops, it must have been almost a religious experience to emerge from the "The Wilderness," as did Moses, and actually see the "Promised Land." As the troops entered Greenupsburg, they picked up their step and began to march, not as a weary exhausted army in retreat, but as an army on parade walking with a "firm, steady tread into the little village of Greenupsburg as though they had rested for a full month."[16]

The Little Sandy River empties into the Ohio River here. Ohio is in the background. Photograph taken by Lewis D. Nicholls.

George Morgan sent a small detachment ahead into the village of Greenupsburg to notify the inhabitants that an army of 10,000 Union soldiers was about to enter the town. Morgan realized that the soldiers were scantily clad because their clothes had literally worn off their bodies. Many of the soldiers had no shoes, pants, or shirts, so they marched in ranks in their underwear. "The women of Greenupsburg were requested to stay indoors or leave the town until we had crossed the river, as our army was literally naked and unfit to be seen by the eyes of a respectable community."[17] This army looked like a bunch of beggars.[18]

On Friday, October 3, 1862, at 2 p.m. the Twenty-sixth Brigade marched into Greenup.[19] For the first time since they had left Cumberland Gap, the Federal troops felt that they were appreciated as soldiers trying to preserve the Union instead of conquerors entering an occupied territory.[20] One father took his little girl by the hand and led her outside of their house. The little girl began to wave a small Stars and Stripes flag as the 42nd Ohio marched through town.[21] The townsfolk began to come out of their houses and cheer the Union column as they marched through town. The Union soldiers "marched into Greenupsburg in as good order and with as firm a step as men fresh from a long rest and a well supplied encampment. Their bare feet and their torn clothes indicated a hard, rough march, but the step, the eye and the fine movement gave proof of good discipline, good order, and the true stamina of the soldier."[22]

William Warner Reid of the 16th Ohio stated, "The people treated us very kindly, for which we were very thankful, having marched 13 miles this day."[23] *The Cincinnati Daily Gazette* reporter stated in his column describing the scene, "A little further on the ladies [of Greenup] brought water from the well, and in person waited on the tired soldiery. Arriving in town we soon found that the ladies were baking bread — not ordinary loaves, but nice fine cakes such as Kentucky ladies delight to spread before chosen guests. One day — a Mrs. Rose — baked more than two hundred pounds of fine flour; and then, as though regretful that it was not better, spread it out before the 26th Brigade, anxious still to do more."[24] It is noteworthy to point out that the 22nd Kentucky was a regiment of the 26th Brigade. Companies B, C and part of F of the 22nd Kentucky were comprised of men recruited from Greenup County.[25] No wonder the ladies of Greenup treated these soldiers like royalty; many of them may have been their own sons!

Although most of the soldiers were grateful for the royal treatment and acted as gentlemen, Private Owen Johnston Hopkins of the 42nd Ohio reported, "The town was ransacked by the voracious soldiers, but not enough was obtained to appease our hunger."[26] However, hungry soldiers ransacking the town seemed incompatible with the description of the events by the Gazette reporter's account. What most likely happened was that some of the soldiers got into some alcoholic beverages that went immediately to their brains on empty stomachs. When the good ladies of Greenup ran out of loaves of bread and other culinary delights, some of the drunken soldiers got rowdy in their pursuit of something to eat.

Morgan ordered the troops to make camp in and around Greenup that first night on October 3, 1862. The soldiers must have been weary and just simply collapsed.

The imbedded reporter with the *Cincinnati Daily Gazette* attached to the 26th Brigade decided he wanted to travel to Cincinnati as soon as possible. He walked down to the wharf, along the banks of the Ohio River at Greenup, and hired a boatman to take him to Portsmouth, Ohio, that evening. The reporter had six in his party that wanted to go to Portsmouth twenty miles below Greenup. He figured that the party of six could then board a steamer at Portsmouth and be in Cincinnati by the next day. The boatman and the reporter agreed upon a definite time to meet at the wharf. The party of six arrived and waited for one hour after the appointed time, but no boatman appeared. Disappointed, they finally realized that the boatman was not going to show and their moonlight ride to Portsmouth, Ohio, was not going to occur.

A young man was at the Greenup wharf and saw their situation. He offered them a ride across the river in his boat to his hometown of Haverhill, Ohio that very evening for five dollars. From Haverhill he would take them to Portsmouth in a wagon. The reporter and his friends accepted the offer. Once they landed on the Ohio side of the River, the party expected to find a wagon waiting on them. Instead, the young man told them that they must walk to his house a short distance away. Several in the party of six were ill and footsore from the ordeal of marching approximately 200 miles through the mountains of eastern Kentucky. Naturally, they began to complain and told the young man that they were not going to pay him if he didn't live up to his end of the bargain. The young man looked at them, grunted, then walked on towards his house. Then the party of six weary travelers really began to complain, believing that they were shabbily treated by the Ohioan. Suddenly, they came upon a stately house illuminated by the dim light of the silver autumn moon.

The Ohioan escorted the party through the garden, into the plaza, and invited them to have a seat while they waited for the wagon. "In a few minutes a half dozen fine ladies were waiting on us and all were enjoying the luxury of champagne. Then came the invitation for supper. The kindness of the Kentucky ladies had not wholly deprived us of our appetites, and we said we were not unwilling to eat a little more. And then such a table was spread. The cloth and bread so white. The pies, cake and sweet meats. The tea, the coffee, the sweet milk and the buttermilk are tempting. Many began to 'calculate' how long it had been since they had seen such a table; and one young man began to question whether his state of health would admit even his sitting at such a table: And to cap the climax, the old gentlemen brought out a pail full of most excellent cider with which to douse ourselves while the ladies were perfecting their display. We drank cider that reached just the spot that had become weak, and wanted one."[27]

It didn't take long before the champagne and cider (we can safely assume that the cider was hard) caused these men to drink a toast to the heroes of Cumberland Gap, the ladies of Haverhill, the ladies of Greenupsburg, the 7th Division, the 26th Brigade, the Union, Abe Lincoln, etc. It must have been quite a night of celebration! The young man from Haverhill must have had quite a ride in his wagon the rest of the night as he drove them to Portsmouth to catch the steamer.[28]

George Morgan knew that the 7th Division had to cross the Ohio River. He sent two captains, Garber and Patterson, across the river to make arrangements for the transportation of the Division.[29]

The next day, October 4, 1862, Morgan ordered the 26th Brigade to march five miles downriver to a location described by Private William Warner Reid of Company C, 16th Ohio Infantry, as Reid's Landing.[30] The 26th Brigade embarked on steamers and barges. They traveled downstream to Wheelersburg, Ohio and then debarked during a heavy rain shower. The soldiers "marched into town where we found a nice dinner prepared for our Brigade."[31] In Wheelersburg the soldiers found that ladies from the surrounding towns of southern Ohio had pooled their resources to feed the hungry soldiers. Private Owen Johnston Hopkins of the 42nd Ohio Vol. Regiment described the scene as follows:

> The citizens [of Wheelersburg] were aroused, and scouring the country in every direction, succeeded in accumulating at Wheelersburg, on the Ohio side of the river, a repast for the hungry men. Now for the first time in months, we marched to the step of martial music through a loyal town with loyal inhabitants, in whose breasts loyal sympathies were beating and whose tears were shed for our suffering boys. Out beyond the village, upon the open common, a repast was spread for us, and never before was a repast so relished. We devoured roasted meats and pies, cakes, and every good thing that loyal and true hands had provided, like famished wolves. Men and women stood crying to see how near starving we had been. Every little article was asked for from us as relics, and even our tin plates which we had used for graters were begged of us for keepsakes. Such evident loyalty and love of the soldier by these dear people were highly appreciated by us, and we even parted with pieces of our garments to satisfy their requests. Anything we could do in return for their great kindness, was done willingly. A bevy of young ladies with baskets of pies and cookies and other delicacies besieged me for a tin spoon which I had carried from the Gap. I gave it to the prettiest one in the group; to another, I gave a piece of leather cut from my cartridge-box belt.[32]

Morgan also ordered Colonel Byrd, commander of the First

Tennessee Regiment, to cross the Ohio River. The wagons and artillery of the 24th Brigade and 27th Brigade were ferried over on large barges. The horses were made to ford or swim.[33] Eventually, the rest of the Division was ferried over the Ohio River to Wheelersburg, Ohio. While one regiment was ferried, the remaining soldiers in Greenup would write letters, rest, and relax after their arduous ordeal until the entire Division was safely in Ohio.

The soldiers first heard that they would be traveling to Camp Dennison, Ohio, near northeast Cincinnati for refitting. But, any orders issued for Camp Dennison were soon countermanded. The Division marched instead, to Sciotodale, present day Sciotoville, and boarded railroad cars. The railroad cars transported the regiments of the Division to Portland, Ohio, about one mile from Oak Hill, Ohio. The Division remained at Portland, Ohio, until October 22, 1862, when they received orders to proceed to Gallipolis, Ohio. The U.S. Army issued them additional supplies such as tents and other necessities at Gallipolis. There were insufficient supplies for the entire Division, so not every regiment obtained the items they needed. This type of bureaucratic bungling added to the suffering of the 7th Division, especially as colder weather began to set in.

On October 25, 1862, the Division proceeded to Point Pleasant, Virginia (present day West Virginia). The next day, they traveled up the Kanawha Valley to Charleston, West Virginia. They stayed near Charleston for two weeks, then headed down the Kanawha River until they came out at the Ohio River again. From here the 24th Brigade went on into western Virginia while the rest of the Division was ordered down the Ohio River, with stops at Cincinnati and Louisville, until they hit the Mississippi and eventually on to Vicksburg. Later the regiments of the 7th Division distinguished themselves in the Battle of Vicksburg.

The nation seemed genuinely glad that the 7th Division was safe and, for the most part, intact. Newspaper articles congratulated

General Morgan and the 7th Division on their historic withdrawal from certain death. The regiments of the 7th Division would live to fight another day. But, the Battle of Perryville, Kentucky, on October 8, 1862, overshadowed the 7th Division's accomplishments. The soldiers of the 7th Division endured a very difficult march for seventeen days over some of the most rugged terrain in the Union. The 7th Division inflicted over 500 casualties on the Confederate forces during their occupation of Cumberland Gap, yet lost only 80 men in the withdrawal across eastern Kentucky. But, not everybody in Washington saw the withdrawal as a victory that saved 10,000 Union soldiers from certain destruction.

Chapter 17
Principles of War & Morgan's Leadership Skills

Initially politicians in Washington praised General Morgan for taking Cumberland Gap without the loss of a single Union soldier. Their praise turned to criticism, however, after Morgan evacuated the Gap in late September and early October. They criticized him for attacking Cumberland Gap when he was ordered to pull back and not take any unnecessary risks in the June 11, 1862, message from General Buell. Was their criticism justified?

The United States Army recognizes nine principles of war.[1] The Army teaches these principles as follows:

Objective. Every military operation must be directed toward a clearly defined, decisive, and attainable objective. The ultimate military objective of war is the destruction of the enemy's armed forces and his will to fight. The objective of each operation must contribute to this ultimate objective. Each intermediate objective must be such that its attainment will most directly, quickly, and economically contribute to the purpose of the operation. The selection of an objective is based upon consideration of the means available, the enemy, and the area of operations. Every commander must understand and clearly define his objective and consider each contemplated action in light thereof.

Offensive. Offensive action is necessary to achieve decisive results and to maintain freedom of action. It permits the commander to exercise initiative and impose his will upon the enemy; to set the pace and determine the course of battle; to exploit enemy weaknesses and rapidly changing situations, and to meet unexpected developments. The defensive may be forced on the commander, but it should be deliberately adopted only as a temporary expedient while awaiting an opportunity for offensive action or for the purpose of economizing forces on a front where a decision is not sought. Even on the defensive the commander seeks every opportunity to seize the initiative and achieve decisive results by offensive action.

Mass. Superior combat power must be concentrated at the critical time and place for a decisive purpose. Superiority results from the proper combination of the elements of combat power. Proper application of the principle of mass, in conjunction with the other principles of war, may permit numerically inferior forces to achieve decisive combat superiority.

Economy of Force. Skillful and prudent use of combat power will enable the commander to accomplish the mission with minimum expenditure of resources. This principle is the corollary of the principle of mass. It does not imply husbanding but rather the measured allocation of available combat power to the primary task as well as secondary tasks such as limited attacks, the defense, deception, or even retrograde action in order to insure sufficient combat power at the point of decision.

Maneuver. Maneuver is an essential ingredient of combat power. It contributes materially in exploiting successes and in preserving freedom of action and reducing vulnerability. The object of maneuver is to dispose a force in such a manner as to place the enemy at a relative disadvantage and thus achieve results which would otherwise be more costly at a relative disadvantage and thus achieve results which would otherwise be more costly in men and materiel. Successful maneuver requires flexibility in organization, administrative support, and command and control. It is the antithesis of permanence of location and implies avoidance of stereotyped patterns of operation.

Unity of Command. The decisive application of full combat power requires unity of command. Unity of command obtains unity of effort by the coordinated action of all forces toward a common goal. While coordination may be attained by cooperation, it is best achieved by vesting a single commander with the requisite authority.

Security. Security is essential to the preservation of combat power. Security is achieved by measures taken to prevent surprise, preserve freedom of action, and deny the enemy information of friendly forces. Since risk is inherent in war, application of the principle of security does not imply undue caution and the avoidance of calculated risk. Security frequently is enhanced by bold seizure and retention of the initiative, which denies the enemy the opportunity to interfere.

Surprise. Surprise can decisively shift the balance of combat power. By surprise, success out of proportion to the effort expended may be obtained. Surprise results from striking an enemy at a time, place, and in a manner for which he is not prepared. It is not essential that the enemy be taken unaware but only that he becomes aware too late to react effectively. Factors contributing to surprise include speed, deception, application of unexpected combat power, effective intelligence and counterintelligences, to include communication and electronic security, and variations in tactics and methods of operation.

Simplicity. Simplicity contributes to successful operations. Direct, simple plans and the simplest plan is preferred.[2]

With the advantage of twenty-twenty hindsight, we can analyze General Morgan's handling of the military situation as commander during the Cumberland Gap operation in June 1862. He concentrated on one military objective that was, of course, the seizure of Cumberland Gap. This was a clearly defined and attainable objective. General Buell ordered him to take and hold the Gap, and that is exactly what he did!

General Morgan utilized offensive action in taking the Gap, and the Confederates maintained the static position by trying to hold the Gap. This gave Morgan the freedom of action necessary to impose his will on the defenders. He exploited enemy weaknesses by taking advantage of the relatively undefended positions at Rogers and Big Creek Gaps. Thus, he was able to lead the 7th Division through these relatively undefended gaps encountering little enemy resistance, but with great physical hardship to his troops who marched over the mountains. But more importantly the 7th Division suffered no loss of life. He responded to the unexpected report that the Confederates had abandoned the Gap by ordering his troops back over the mountains the third time to take advantage of the rapidly changing conditions as the Confederates abandoned Cumberland Gap.

Morgan massed his four brigades at the base of Rogers Gap, once he was on the southern side of the Cumberland Mountains. He positioned his artillery near the front of the two columns so they could be brought to bear quickly on any enemy resistance. Hence, Morgan effectively used the principle of mass in seizing the Gap.

Morgan maneuvered his troops through the two gaps, greatly

reducing the exposure of the 7th Division to vulnerability. After he took Cumberland Gap, Morgan estimated that he would have lost two-thirds of his Division if he had attempted a frontal assault. Morgan's application of the principle of maneuver resulted in obtaining his objective without the loss of a single soldier.

Morgan was vested with the required authority to make all decisions during the June 1862 operation. His four brigade commanders understood who was in charge, and Morgan orchestrated his brigades to direct their coordinated efforts toward the common goal of seizing the Gap.

Morgan was also very security minded. On the two roads towards Rogers Gap and Big Creek Gap, he directed his engineers to build roads toward the front of the column. However, he had another contingent of engineers behind the column tearing up the road so that a Confederate patrol could not surprise them from behind. In fact, Morgan was rarely surprised in a tactical situation because he positioned pickets and was security minded at all times. Thus, Morgan adhered to the principle of security.

Morgan also feinted at the front of the Gap by keeping enough troops, even some disabled troops, parading around in an ostentatious manner to make the Confederates believe the main body of the 7th Division was at Pineville. This feint occurred while the main Union body was crossing Rogers Gap and Big Creek Gap. By the time the Confederates figured out that Morgan was not at Pineville, the 7th Division was behind them. Thus, Morgan effectively used the principle of surprise.

Morgan's plan to proceed east and cross Rogers and Big Creek Gaps, rendezvous at the base of Rogers Gap, and proceed to the Gap was a simple plan. Morgan's legal training as an attorney served him well as he scrutinized his written orders with the skill of an attorney writing a contract weighing each word for precision and clarity. This approach resulted in clear and concise orders, minimizing misunderstanding and confusion.

Clearly, Morgan did it right as he commanded the 7th Division in the attack on Cumberland Gap during June 1862. He correctly applied all of the principles of war as recognized by today's U.S. Army, and he certainly did not deserve the criticism he received for this operation.

What kind of leader was General George Washington Morgan? What kind of leadership characteristics did he possess? First, he gave credit to subordinate officers for jobs well done. For example, in his official report to Congress after taking Cumberland Gap in June 1862, he stated that, ". . . I must mention, in terms of commendations, Lieutenant Colonel Reuben Munday, with his battalion of Kentucky cavalry."[3] He also stated,

"The highest praise is also due to my personal staff, for their unremitting devotion to the interests of the service, and I therefore commend Captain C. O. Johne, assistant adjutant general, chief of staff: Captain S. S. Lyon, acting topographical engineer; Major M. C. Garber, division quartermaster, and Captain G. M. Adams, C. S., for the immense aid they have given me during the period of my command; and had their services been less zealous and and efficient, I could not have advanced.."[4]

General Morgan praised his quartermaster located in Lexington, Kentucky, who he felt performed the duties of three men.[5] He praised Lieutenant H. G. Fisher, his signal corps officer, by stating, "He has always been efficient, and his telegraphic line has nearly kept pace with the advance of my column."[6] General Morgan repeated the same pattern of giving credit to subordinate officers and men in his report on the evacuation of Cumberland Gap later that fall. Morgan's brigade commanders, in turn, praised their officers and men in their reports. Managers praising subordinates for jobs well done has long been considered good leadership technique.[7]

General Morgan also valued the life of each individual sol-dier. He did not recklessly order his troops to charge forward straight into Cumberland Gap, which he estimated would have cost him two-thirds of his command.[8] The maneuver of his troops around the well defended Cumberland Gap caused him to take the objective without the loss of any men. Morgan commented in his report that, "The result secured by strategy is less brilliant than a victory obtained amid the storm and hurricane of battle; but humanity has gained all that glory has lost, and I am satisfied."[9]

There is an old adage in the Army that you can delegate au-thority, but not responsibility. This means that commanders may consult with subordinate commanders and elicit opinions from them on the best course of action to follow; however the commander has to make the call and be responsible for the consequences of the decision he makes. The commander cannot blame the decision on another individual for advice that the other individual may give if the result goes sour. Morgan understood this principle as illustrated in his com-ment in his report that,

I had now at the foot of Roger's gap the brigades of Baird and DeCourcy, and as the valley was occupied by the enemy's cavalry, I ordered the supply trains to the rear, and was compelled to subsist upon the foe. I felt all the responsibility of my position, for I had adopted my plan of operations contrary to the opinions of three of my brigade commanders, all of whom I hold in high esteem.[10]

Apparently, Morgan consulted his commanders about the best tactical formation they should employ once they crossed Rogers and Big Creek Gaps and proceeded toward Cumberland Gap. Morgan also used this same type of consulting leadership style to determine the best course of action to follow in deciding if he should evacuate Cumberland Gap.[11] Morgan surrounded himself with subordinate commanders whom he trusted as competent officers, elicited and considered their opinions, made the decision and then assumed responsibility for it.

Morgan was not afraid to make a decision. He made the decision to order his troops back across Rogers Gap the third time when he received information that the Confederates had abandoned Cumberland Gap. This was a risky decision since his troops had already crossed Rogers Gap twice and were no doubt fatigued. If the Confederates caught them in a fatigued state, a route of the Union troops would have been easier to obtain. It was also risky because he had to read a poorly written message from General Buell and infer that Buell had given him the authority, at his discretion, to attack Cumberland Gap. If General Morgan had attacked Cumberland Gap and failed to take it, then he would have jeopardized his military as well as future career.

Morgan was an excellent general because of his military knowledge, his communication skills, his willingness to consider his brigade commander's tactical opinions, his motivation skills, and his concern for the well being of his troops. General Morgan's excellent leadership characteristics and military competence served him well during his tenure as a military leader and during the trials that followed.

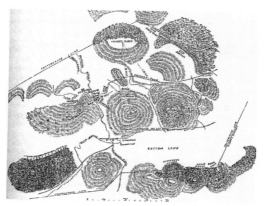

Plan of the Confederate works at Cumberland Gap, June 14, 1865. From a drawing by Captain W. F. Patterson. *Battles and Leaders of the Civil War, Volume III.*

Chapter 18
Epilogue

General George Washington Morgan was a competent military commander; however, his competence did not protect him from being caught up in Washington politics. General Don Carlos Buell commanded the Army of the Ohio, and George Morgan was one of his division commanders. This relationship was very unfortunate for George Morgan because Secretary of War Edwin M. Stanton, and his Chief of Staff, General Henry W. Halleck, decided to fire General Buell after the Battle of Perryville. Buell's slow, deliberate pace in conducting military operations just didn't suit Stanton or Halleck who demanded that Buell bring them a major military victory immediately. Although Buell's slow deliberate pace in the western theater allowed the Confederates to escape a major military defeat during 1862, for political reasons, Washington needed a major military victory during 1862 because congressional elections were just around the corner.

Buell received orders on October 30, 1862, relieving him of command of the Army of the Ohio. He relinquished command to General William S. Rosecrans. Secretary of War, Edwin M. Stanton, advised Lincoln that relieving Buell was the best policy because Buell failed to obtain significant military victories. Stanton did not consider

Perryville a significant military victory because Buell had failed to destroy the combined armies of Braxton Bragg and Kirby Smith. Buell did succeed, however, in causing the Confederate forces to withdraw from Kentucky never to return, except for a few minor raids by Confederate commanders such as John Hunt Morgan. But, "congressional elections were near; and Midwestern Republicans demanded defeat of the enemy lest the party lose prestige." [1]

Many northern newspapers and politicians began to publicly blame Buell for the Union's lack of significant military victories. They impugned his "character and his loyalty and [undermined] his reputation as a professional soldier." [2] Buell believed that his removal was for political reasons, so he demanded that Secretary of War, Edwin Stanton, appoint a court of inquiry to "exonerate himself from the public execution that he suffered in the press and to reclaim a favorable reputation." [3] Stanton agreed and appointed a six-member panel as a board of inquiry. On December 1, 1862, the court of inquiry began. It lasted for five months and was for the purpose of determining if there existed sufficient evidence to court-martial General Buell.

The Buell Commission, as it was called, was really a political "witch hunt" looking for a scapegoat because of the Union's lack of spectacular battlefield successes. "The trial ended in early May 1863 after more than five months of courtroom combat, which included daily sessions of grueling testimony of over seventy witnesses in three cities." [4] The Commission concluded that, "despite being slow, unaggressive, inflexible, sympathetic to southerners and slavery, and not in harmony with the government's aims for waging or winning war, Buell could not be charged with any crime or misconduct that warranted court-martial." [5]

The Buell Commission spelled bad news for General George Morgan. After all, George Morgan was the commander who had lost Cumberland Gap. But, what was really on trial was the philosophy of how the war should be waged.

Buell believed that the southern soldier was better disciplined than the Union soldier. He believed that it was necessary to drill constantly to prepare for battle. Buell also believed it was better to maneuver than to use brute force to gain the objective. Consequently, the Buell Commission accused Buell of lack of aggressiveness citing these attributes as proof.

Interestingly enough, Morgan demonstrated that he was an aggressive fighter. He captured Cumberland Gap in June 1862 by bypassing a frontal assault and slipping in behind the Confederates through Big Creek and Roger's Gaps. When Morgan received an order capable of being interpreted in two different ways — one to fall back and one to proceed forward — Morgan chose to interpret it as approval to proceed forward and capture Cumberland Gap.

Morgan requested permission from Buell to proceed on into eastern Tennessee and disrupt the rail lines after he captured Cumberland Gap. However, Buell told Morgan to remain at the Gap and not to proceed further into Tennessee.

Morgan took the initiative during the march to Greenup by placing many of his troops in the front and on the flanks to prevent surprise attacks. Not only was Morgan complying with the principle of security, but this tactical deployment also exhibited military aggressiveness desired by the Buell Commission. Yet, the Commission punished Morgan for his aggressiveness by making him defend himself before the tribunal.

The Commission accused Buell of being sympathetic to the Southern cause because Buell issued orders to treat southern soldiers as enemies and southern civilians as loyal Union citizens until they proved otherwise. This policy did not set well with Stanton and the Commission because they insisted on a policy of total war. Buell reasoned that since his soldiers would have to subsist off the land while on campaigns, it made sense to treat the civilian population well by not stealing their food or needlessly destroying their property. This policy made a lot of sense in eastern Tennessee where the majority of the inhabitants supported the Union. However, in central Tennessee the population was not as supportive of the Union. With civilian assistance, the Rebels cut Buell's supply trains during his attempted march to Chattanooga so severely that Buell withdrew back into Kentucky.

If Morgan adhered to a philosophy of reconciliation with the Confederates, he certainly did not demonstrate it. While he occupied Cumberland Gap, he repeatedly sent foraging expeditions into eastern Tennessee looking for food and supplies. Morgan approved of taking all of the chickens, pigs, corn, etc., his troops could find during the march to Greenup. In summary, the Buell Commission stymied a commander who shared the Commission's own philosophy of war.

The Buell Commission also chastised Buell for being sympathetic to slavery.[6] One of the reasons George Morgan resigned his commission in 1863 was because he opposed using African American men as soldiers.[7] Once again, the Commission stomped on a Union officer who shared its philosophy. This was truly a case of the Union "eating its own young." If Buell saw the tribunal as an opportunity to clear his name, George Morgan saw it as an unfair and unjustified inquiry into his leadership abilities distracting him from more important duties.

George Morgan had practiced law before the Civil War, and he was not going to be intimidated or bullied by the Administration into being their "scapegoat." On December 6, 1862, Morgan wrote a letter to Adjutant-General Loreno Thomas, acting adjutant for General Halleck, at Division Headquarters in Memphis, Tennessee, requesting " a copy of the charges and specifications preferred against me."[8] He then gave them a list of the witnesses he desired to have summoned. This placed the War Department on notice that they had a fight on their hands if they were trying to make George Morgan a "scapegoat." As an attorney George Morgan knew how to play the courtroom game! He was no ordinary general.

In late August 1862, the War Department had reorganized the Department of the Ohio military district. The reorganization basically stripped Buell of command while his troops were in Kentucky. "The new Kentucky jurisdiction fell to Gen. Horatio G. Wright, who was in Cincinnati."[9] General Wright was then General Buell's commander.

On October 15, 1862, General Wright wrote a report in which he attached a copy of George Morgan's report of the evacuation of Cumberland Gap. General Wright stated in the report, "It appears from this report [Morgan's report] that the evacuation, which was in pursuance of the unanimous opinion of a council of the general officers of the command, was a matter of necessity, arising from their provisions being exhausted, their communications cut off, and on information of any prospect of relief being received. While the evacuation of the Gap is to be regretted, I do not see how, with starvation staring him in the face and with no certainty of relief being afforded, he could have come to any other conclusion than the one arrived at."[10] With this kind of endorsement from General Wright, it is inconceivable that the Buell Commission plunged forward trying to blame George Morgan with incompetence by abandoning Cumberland Gap. However, they plunged forward anyway!

What is even more incredible is that the Buell Commission decided to investigate George Morgan's conduct as a commander without even telling Morgan. On or about December 6, 1862, General Morgan received notice that the Buell Commission had not only set its sights on Buell, but on Morgan as well. When Morgan learned of this, he wrote a letter to General Halleck dated December 6, 1862, requesting to be relieved from his command, and that a court of inquiry or court-martial be initiated.[11] On December 20, 1862, General Halleck responded to General Morgan stating, "I am directed to say that Major-General Wright was directed some time since to investigate and report the facts concerning that affair. If that report should be satisfactory to the War Department no further proceedings will be required, and you will be relieved from all blame."[12] Halleck responded to Morgan in this manner knowing full well two months earlier that General Wright had absolved General Morgan of any blame for abandoning Cumberland Gap. Finally, on February 8, 1863, Halleck wrote a letter to General Wright acknowledging that Wright had written him absolving Morgan of making a military blunder. In this letter, Halleck continued to blame Morgan for passing incorrect information to his higher command causing them to believe that the 7th Division's plight at Cumberland was not as bad as it really was.[13] What was Halleck's motivation in trying to make Morgan look like his decision in abandoning Cumberland Gap was a military blunder? The motivation could be summed up in one word — politics. In order to hold onto congressional seats in the upcoming elections, the Republicans needed a scapegoat to blame for the lack of Union military victories during 1862.

The public immediately saw through this deception. John Van Buren, from the Cooper Institute of New York, wrote a speech that appeared in many newspapers through out the nation including the Ironton Register of October 23, 1862. In this article, Van Buren stated, "I pronounce the retreat right and proper; and I assert that it was conducted with a skill and daring which entitle Gen. Morgan and his officers and men under his command to the highest honors. Still, I hold that the court ought to be called and if I were a member of Congress I would urge its call, not to look into Gen. Morgan's conduct but to indict, try, and punish the Government of the United States and the army authorities for making the retreat necessary, and for leaving so gallant an army for so many months surrounded destitute of clothes, provisions and money where the facts were made known to the authorities at Washington and they were implored to send this army relief."[14]

In 1866 the historian J. T. Headley wrote in his two volume

series, *The Great Rebellion*, "By his foresight, energy and indomitable perseverance, he [Morgan] escaped from the trap in which an inefficient General-in-Chief [Halleck] had allowed him to be caught,. . . Instead, however, of congratulating him on his skill and success, in his report sent into Congress the following winter, Halleck had the injustice to censure him for evacuating the Gap, saying that 'an investigation had been ordered.' . . . That the latter [Halleck] should be guilty of the gross injustice of casting censure on a brave officer, in order to cover up his own short-comings, is perhaps not surprising; but that he should put on record statements, which, placed side by side, present him in such a painful aspect to the public is certainly very remarkable. The whole campaign as planned, was a palpable blunder, and it was natural that he should put the blame of failure upon some one else; but this mode of doing it admits of no excuse."[15]

Even the lowest private in the ranks of Morgan's Division knew that Halleck had mistreated Morgan and the entire 7th Division when Pvt. Owen Johnston Hopkins of the 42nd Ohio Vol. Regiment stated, "The overwhelming enemy continued to draw closer and closer around us every day, narrowing our field for forage until, at length, starvation began to stare us in the face. The men looked lank and haggard from hunger and exposure, and were almost worn out by arduous duties in the chill mountain air at night, and as no man amongst the privates possessed a full suit of clothing, suffering from cold was added to that of hunger. What was to be done? Answer, you who harped so incessantly on Morgan's 'disgraceful abandonment' of Cumberland Gap! Or perhaps the Military Commission before whom General Morgan was tried for neglect of duty, could now answer?"[16]

The Confederate response to George Morgan's withdrawal of the 7th Division from Cumberland Gap several years later in retrospect was even more poignant than the Union reaction. Colonel Vance commanded one of Confederate General Stephenson's brigades as they attempted to cut off the 7th Division at Cumberland Gap. In 1864 Colonel Vance wrote a letter to General George Morgan in which Vance stated that the Gap would have been surrounded and entirely cut off had the Confederates had only an additional forty-eight (48) hours. The entire 7th Division would have been captured had not Morgan abandoned Cumberland Gap when he did. Colonel Vance stated in his letter that, "It was the opinion of every officer of rank in our army that you moved at exactly the proper time, and with great skill and judgment."[17]

The Confederate high command also had an opinion about the events at Cumberland Gap. Confederate General Braxton Bragg stated in his official report at the close of the Kentucky campaign:

Orders had also been given for a close observation of the enemy at Cumberland Gap, and that he should be intercepted in any attempt to escape. On my arrival at Bardstown, I learned from Gen. Smith that the enemy was moving from Cumberland Gap endeavoring to escape by the valley of the Sandy River in Eastern Kentucky, and that he had sent his whole available force in pursuit, a sufficient force to prevent this escape and compel the enemy's surrender, had been ordered and confidently expected from another quarter to have followed Gen. Smith's movements in time for this purpose. Circumstances in the then isolated position, and over which I could not control, had prevented this consummation so confidently relied on, and so necessary to success. The delay resulting from this pursuit of the enemy by Gen. Smith, prevented a junction of your forces and enabled Gen. Buell to reach Louisville before the assault could be made upon that city.[18]

General Bragg obviously felt that the pursuit of George Morgan and the 7th Division delayed the massing of Confederate forces for a sufficient amount of time to allow Union General Buell's army to escape the Confederate pursuit. This allowed Buell enough time to pull back to Louisville, Kentucky, and regroup, eventually leading to the Union victory at Perryville and ultimate Confederate withdrawal back to Tennessee.

Historians from the Twentieth century have viewed General Halleck's insistence to prosecute Generals Don Carlos Buell and George Washington Morgan as disingenuous. Mr. Artus James writes in his doctoral thesis, "That this retreat should have been the subject of a Board of Inquiry seems incredible. Yet such was the case. The evidence seemed to clear General Morgan of all blame, though General Halleck's acquittal seemed very ungracious, probably because he was somewhat responsible for the failure to send reinforcements which rendered retreat a necessity."[19]

General George Washington Morgan did not deserve the treatment given to him by General Halleck over abandoning Cumberland Gap. The expedition and occupation of the Gap was based upon arcane military principles no longer applicable during this—the first modern war.

B. F. Stevenson, surgeon of the 22nd Kentucky Infantry, stated, "I think there is a history of the expedition yet to be written which will change the opinions of the world as to its importance, and the policy on which it was based. That it has failed in its original design is now manifest to all; and the causes leading to that failure when they come to be investigated, will, I think, vindicate the propriety of Gen. Morgan's action."[20] Union war planners intended that the occupation of Cumberland Gap was to guard the traditional route into Kentucky from Tennessee along the Wildness Road. If an army could hold Cumberland Gap, then it could deny the other army access into either Tennessee or Kentucky. The fallacy with this thinking was that holding the Gap no longer prevented an army from crossing the Cumberland Mountains through other passes. During the month of June 1862, the Confederates held Cumberland Gap. However, George Morgan and the 7th Division crossed the Cumberland Mountain range by coming through Big Creek and Rogers Gaps. Morgan proved that holding Cumberland Gap was an exercise in futility. It tied down 10,000 troops that could have been used in other places, such as Perryville.

Not only was Cumberland Gap's strategic importance diminished to minuscule importance, but also it was impossible to supply twelve months of the year because of poor roads. Thus, the Union's obsession with trying to hold it was based on two false premises. First, holding the Gap would not prevent armies from entering Tennessee or Kentucky. Second, positions held at the Gap could not be adequately supplied due to inadequate roads. An army may have been able to take Cumberland Gap, but it simply could not hold it year round. Union war planners failed to grasp these two concepts.

The Union surgeon, B. F. Stevenson stated, "The brightest feather in Gen. Morgan's plume was won in the retreat from Cumberland Gap. In a fight, audacity and dash often accomplish wonders. A retreat, however, tests a man's mettle. This one was accomplished, amid many difficulties, with prudence, circumspection, and unflagging energy." [21] The 7th Division demonstrated steadiness under fire honed by steadfast discipline. Morgan made the correct decision in withdrawing from Cumberland Gap under the circumstances. Any competent battlefield commander would have done the same thing. The treatment Morgan and his men received from the Administration was unwarranted, disgraceful, and did a real disservice to the reputation of this excellent fighting unit.

Some historians have stated that the best of the U.S. Army officers joined the Confederacy explaining why it took so long for the Union to win the war. Many good officers did go to the South, but just as many good officers remained loyal to the Union. The problem was a mediocre Union high command that didn't understand that they were in a different kind of war. This war called for a different set of tactics and strategies from the other wars America had previously fought. The Union won the Civil War in spite of leaders such as Halleck because of officers like George Washington Morgan and the unflagging devotion to duty of his officer corps and enlisted men. Their story has now been told! Finally, General Morgan's actions at Cumberland Gap have now been vindicated, and the reputation of his officers and men are now untarnished!

Notes

Chapter 1
Political Situation

1. Kincaid, Robert L., *The Wilderness Road* (Arcata Graphics, 1992), 27.
2. Ibid., 27.
3. Ibid., 47-48.
4. Ibid., 49.
5. The New Encyclopaedia Britannica, Volume III, page 291 (1974)
6. Harrison, Lowell H., *The Civil War in Kentucky* (The University Press of Kentucky, 1975), 9
7. McDonough, James Lee, *War in Kentucky from Shiloh to Perryville,* (The University of Tennessee Press/ Knoxville, 1994), 61 (Quoting historian James McPherson)
8. Harrison, *The Civil War in Kentucky*, 2.
9. Noe, Kenneth W., *Perryville: This Grand Havoc of Battle,* (The University Press of Kentucky, 2001), 6.
10. Harrison, *The Civil War in Kentucky*, 11.
11. Noe, *Perryville: This Grand Havoc of Battle*, 7.
12. Harrison, *The Civil War in Kentucky*, 12.
13. Ibid., 6-7.
14. Hafendorfer, Kenneth A., *Mill Springs*, (KH Press, 2001), 20.
15. Harrison, *The Civil War in Kentucky*, 12.
16. Harrison, *The Civil War in Kentucky*, 13.
17. Hafendorfer, *Mill Springs,* 20.
18. Ibid, 22.
19. Ibid, 23.
20. McDonough, *War in Kentucky from Shiloh to Perryville,* 39.
21. McDonough, *War in Kentucky from Shiloh to Perryville,* 39.
22. O.R., vol. 10, pt.2, 315
23. McDonough, *War in Kentucky from Shiloh to Perryville,* 79.
24. Noe, Kenneth W., *Perryville,* 27.
25. Hafendorfer, *Mill Springs,* 26-27
26. Hafendorfer, *Mill Springs,* 593, and O.R. Vol. 4, 409.
27. Harrison, *The Civil War in Kentucky,* 25.
28. Ibid, 27.
29. Ibid, 27.
30. Ibid, 27.
31. O.R. Vol. 10, pt. 2, 315.
32. Ibid, 315.

Chapter 2
Military Situation

1. McDonough, *War in Kentucky from Shiloh to Perryville,* 31.
2. Ibid, 31.
3. Ibid, 16-17.
4. Ibid, 15.
5. Ibid, 32.
6. Ibid, 40.
7. McDonough, *War in Kentucky from Shiloh to Perryville,* 47.
8. O.R. Series 1-Vol 10 (Part II), page 68.
9. General George Washington Morgan was born in Pennsylvania in 1820. At the age of sixteen, he enlisted in the Texas army during the War of Texas Independence from Mexico. After the war he attended West Point in 1841. He left West Point in 1843 and moved to Ohio to practice law. He fought in the American Mexican War with General Winfield Scott. After the Mexican War, he returned to Ohio and practiced law. In 1856 he was appointed United States consul to Marseilles, France. In 1858 he was appointed minister to Portugal until 1861. While in France he studied military tactics at Chalons, France. He returned to the United States at the beginning of the Civil War. On November 21, 1861, Congress appointed him a brigadier general. He later commanded a division in the Vicksburg campaign, and on January 4, 1863 was appointed a corps commander in the new Army of the Mississippi. He later resigned from the army during June 1863 because he disagreed with enlisting black troops and because his health began to fail. He served I the United States Congress from 1867 to 1873.
10. *Morgan, Major General G. W. :*A resolution of the House of Representatives, transmitting Major General g. W. Morgan's report of the occupation of Cumberland Gap. 38th Congress, 1st Session, Ex. Doc. No. 94., page 1.
11. Ibid, 2.
12. Ibid, 2.
13. *The Handbook of Texas Online,* http://www.tsha.utexas.edu/ handbook/online/articles/view/MM/fmo49.html , accessed Nov 2, 2002.
14. O.R. Series 1-Vol. 10 (Part II), page 186, and *Seventh Division, Army of the Ohio,* http://freepages.military.rootsweb.com/ ~us14thkyinfantry/campaings/cumberlandgap.html, accessed Nov 10, 2002.

15. Ibid.

16. Ibid.

17. Kincaid, Robert L., *The Wilderness Road*, (Arcata Graphics, 1992), 239.

18. O.R. Series 1-Vol 10 (Part II), page 186, and *Seventh Division, Army of the Ohio,* http://freepages.military.rootsweb.com/ ~us14thkyinfantry/campaings/cumberlandgap.html, accessed Nov 10, 2002.

19. *Arlington National Cemetery Website,* http://216.239.39.100/ search?a=cache:Oz00w03XsdsC:www.arlingtoncemetery.com/ absalom, accessed Nov 10, 2002..

20. Ibid.

21. Ibid.

22. O.R. Series 1-Vol. 10 (Part II), page 148.

23. O.R. Series 1-Vol. 10 (Part I), 1.

24. *Edmund Kirby Smith Biography,* http://www.civilwarhome.com/ ksmithbio.htm, accessed Dec 7, 2002.

25. *TNGen Web Project Tennesseans in the Civil War, 11th Tennessee Infantry,* http://www.tngenweb.org/civilwar/csainf/csa11.html, accessed Dec 7, 2002.

26. O.R. Series 1-Vol. 10 (Part I), pages 42-45.

27. Ibid, 44.

28. O.R. Series 1-Vol. 10 (Part II), page 142.

Chapter 3
Union Takes Cumberland Gap

1. Morgan, George W., *Major General G. W. Morgan's report of the occupation of Cumberland Gap to Congress.* (38th Congress, 1st Session, Ex. Doc. No. 94, May 27, 1864), 2.

2. Morgan, *Battles & Leaders of the Civil War,* Vol. 3, 63.

3. Morgan, *Report,* 3.

4. Morgan, *Report,* 9.

5. Ibid, 9.

6. Ibid, 9.

7. Ibid, 9.

8. Ibid, 9.

9. Ibid, 16.

10. Ibid, 16.

11. Ibid, 16.

12. Ibid, 16.

13. Ibid, 12.
14. Ibid, 13.
15. Ibid, 14.
16. O.R. Series 1—Vol. 10 (Part I), page 53.
17. 9th Regiment Michigan Infantry 1861-5, http://members.aol.com/dlharvey/9thinf.htm, accessed Jan 5, 2003..
18. O.R. Series 1—Vol. 10 (Part I), page 53.
19. O.R. Series 1—Vol. 10 (Part I), page 54.
20. O.R. Series 1—Vol. 16 Part I), page 702.
21. Kincaid, *The Wilderness Road*, 241.
22. Ibid, 241.

23. Morgan, *Report*, 4.
24. Morgan, *Report*, 5.
25. Morgan, *Report*, 7.
26. Risk, Estelle S., *No More Muffled Hoofbeats,* (Dorrance & Company, Philadelphia)
27. Morgan, *Report*, 5.
28. Morgan, *Battles & Leaders of the Civil War*, 63.

Chapter 4
Union Occupation of Cumberland Gap—Summer 1862

1. *The Civil War in the Cumberland Gap*, http://www.nps.gov/cuga/civilwar.htm, accessed Jan 12, 2003.
2. Ibid.
3. Mosely, J. M., *Gateway to the West*, Part Four—The Civil War: Hostilities, http://homepages.rootsweb.com/~duncanw/gatewayseries/gatewaysestpt4.htm, accessed Jan 12, 2003.
4. *Long Tom,* http://www.nps.gov/cuga/longtonm.htm, accessed Jan 12, 2003.
5. Morgan, George W., *Battles and Leaders of the Civil War,* (Castle, a division of Book Sales, Inc.), 65.
6. O. R. Series 1, Vol., 16 (Part I), page 717.
7. Ibid, pages 835-836.
8. *The Mount Sterling-Pound Gap Road,* http://www.geocities.com/heartland/9999/MountSterlingPoundGapRoad.html, accessed Feb 3, 2003.
9. O.R. Series 1, Vol. 16 (Part I), page 999.
10. *The Mount Sterling-Pound Gap Road,* Ibid.
11. Wiley, Bell Irvin, *The Life of Billy Yank,* (Louisiana State University

Press 2001), 124.

12. Ibid.
13. Ibid.
14. Ibid, 126.
15. Ibid, 127.
16. Ibid, 127 as quoted in H.C. Hawes, *Experiences of a Union Soldier,* (Atlanta, Ill., 1928).
17. Ibid, 127
18. Morgan, George W., *Battles and Leaders of the Civil War,* (Castle, a division of Book Sales, Inc.), 62.
19. *The Memoirs of Paul Grogger – 2nd Tennessee,* 7 http:// home.cinci.rr.com/secondtennessee/grogger.htm, accessed Feb 4, 2003.
20. O. R. Series 1, Vol, 16(Part I), 996.
21. Ibid, 993.
22. Ibid, 1007.
23. *Cincinnati Daily Gazette,* Vol. 74, No. 85, October 6, 1862.
24. *Cincinnati Commercial,* Vol. XXIII, No. 83, Oct. 9, 1862.
25. *The Memoirs of Paul Groggey – 2nd Tennessee,* 8.
26. *Cincinnati Daily Commercial,* Vol. XXXII, No. 81, Oct. 7, 1862; *Cincinnati Commercial,* Vol. XXIII, No. 77, Oct 2, 1862.
27. Noe, Kenneth W., *Perryville,* 110.
28. Morgan, *Battles and Leaders of the Civil War,* 65.
29. Ibid, 67.
30. Ibid, 65.

Chapter 5
The Case for Invading Kentucky in 1862

1. O. R. Vol. 16, pt.2, 733-734.
2. O. R. Vol. 16, pt. 1, 768
3. Ibid, 769.
4. McDonough, *War in Kentucky, 79.*
5. Coulter, E. Merton, *The Civil War and Readjustment In Kentucky,* (The University of North Carolina Press, 1926), 3.
6. Ibid, 4.
7. Kleber, John E., *The Kentucky Encyclopedia,* (The University Press of Kentucky, 1992), 202.
8. Coulter, *The Civil War and Readjustment In Kentucky,* 5.

9. Ibid, 5.
10. Ibid, 7.
11. Ibid, 8.
12. Ibid, 6-7.
13. Ibid, 9.
14. Ibid, 11.
15. Ibid, 15.
16. Ibid, 13.
17. Ibid, 146.
18. Ibid, 150.
19. Ibid, 151.
20. Ibid, 105.
21. Ibid, 216
22. Ibid, 216.
23. Ibid, 216.
24. Ibid, 217.
25. Ibid, 217.
26. Ibid, 219.
27. Ibid, 168
28. Duke, *Reminiscences,* 305.

Chapter 6
Confederate Invasion of Kentucky

1. *B & L, Vol. III,* 600.
2. O. R., Vol. 16, pt. 2, 733-734.
3. McDonough, *War in Kentucky,* 82.
4. O. R., Vol. 16, pt.2, 724.
5. O. R., Vol. 16, pt.2, 734.
6. O. R., Vol. 16, pt.2, 745-746.
7. O. R., Vol. 16, pt.2, 741.
8. Ibid, 741.
9. Ibid, 741.
10. Kleber, John E., *The Kentucky Encyclopedia,* (The University Press of Kentucky, 1992), 478.
11. McDonough, *War in Kentucky from Shiloh to Perryville,* 82.
12. O. R., Vol. 16, pt.2, 751.
13. Ibid, 751.
14. O. R., Vol. 16, pt.2, 752-753.

15. O. R., Vol. 16, pt.2, 751.

16. *B & L*, Vol. 1, 397.

17. Ibid, 4.

18. O. R. Vol. 16, pt.2, 860.

19. The Diary of N. B. Brewer, Company K, 47th Tennessee Infantry Regiment, C.S.A., http://www.michaelragsdale.com/47th/brewer.html, accessed Feb 4, 2003.

20. O. R. Vol. 16,pt. 2, 860.

21. Ibid, 860.

22. Heidler & Heidler, *Encyclopedia of the American Civil War*, 1864; O. R. Vol. 16, pt.1, 734..

23. *B & L*, Vol.3, 46.

24. Ibid

25. Diary of Private Sam Thompson, 1st Texas Battery, July 15, 1862 through August 29, 1862, http://216.239.39.104/search?q=cache:eiMuwoxEDjsJ:lonestar.utsa.edu/rloper/diaries62page, accessed Feb 4, 2003.

26. O. R. Vol., 16, pt 1, 992.

27. Ibid, 992.

28. O. R. Vol., 16, pt. 1, 1007.

29. Ibid, 1007.

30. *B. & L*, Vol. 3, 66.

31. Ibid, 66.

32. *B & L*, Vol. 3, 66.

33. Duke, Basil W., *the Civil War Reminiscences of General Basil W. Duke, C. S. A.* (Cooper Square Press, 2001), 305.

34. *B & L*, Vol. 3, 66.

35. O. R. Vol. 16, pt 1, 957.

36. Ibid, 957.

37. Ibid, 958.

38. *Cincinnati Daily Gazette*, September 16, 1862.

39. *Cincinnati Daily Gazette*, Vol. 74, No. 72, September 20, 1862.

40. O. R. Vol. 16, pt 2, 814-815.

Chapter 7
John Hunt Morgan & Richard Gano

1. Heidler, David & Jeanne, *Encyclopedia*, 1359.

2. Ibid, 1359.

3. Ervin, Robert Edgar, *The John Hunt Morgan Raid of 1863*, (Robert

Edgar Ervin, Kinko's Inc. 2003), xv.

4. Heidler, David & Jeanne, *Encyclopedia,* 1359.
5. Ibid, 1359.
6. Ibid, 1359.
7. Ibid, 1359.
8. Ibid, 1359.
9. O. R., Vol. 16, pt. 2, 733-734.
10. O. R., Vol. 16, pt. 1, 767-770.
11. Thomas, Edison H., *John Hunt Morgan and His Raiders,* (The University Press of Kentucky, 1975.)
12. Brown, Dee Alexander, *Morgan's Raiders,* (Konecky & Konecky, 1959), 122.
13. Ibid, 122.
14. Ibid, 123.
15. Duke, Basil W., *the Civil War Reminiscences of General Basil W. Duke, C.S.A.,* (Cooper Square Press, 2001), 314.
16. Berry, Thomas F., *Four Years with Morgan and Forrest,* (Harlow-Ratliff Co., Okla. City), 130 as quoted in Records and Correspondence Pertaining to the Military Activities of Brigadier-General Richard M. Gano, C.S.A., Volume I, IV. (Raids on the Louisville & Nashville Railroad, August 1862), June 1, 1861 to July 2, 1863, on file at Abilene Christian University, Abilene, Texas.
17. Holland, Cecil Fletcher, *Morgan and his Raiders,* (The MacMillan Co., New York, 1942.), 147 as quoted in Gano's Records, Vol. I, IV.
18. Ibid, An Experience of Six Weeks Among the Soldiers of Generals Kirby Smith and Bragg, The New York Times, Monday, November 24, 1862, page 3.
19. Ibid.
20. *B & L,* Vol. 3, 26.
21. Duke, Basil W., *Morgan's Cavalry,* (The Neale Publishing Co. New York and Washington, 1909), 161.
22. Gano, Personal War Record of Brigadier-General Richard Montgomery Gano, C.S.A., Volume I, VI. (Morgan's Mountain Campaign, unpublished,1910).
23. Ibid and O. R. Vol. 16, pt. 2, 851.
24. Ibid, Gano
25. Ibid, page 94 et seq.
26. *B & L,* Vol. 3, 26.
27. O. R. Vol. 16, pt. 2, 851.
28. Duke, Basil W., *Reminiscences,* 314.
29. Ibid, xv.
30. Coulter, Merton E., *The Civil War and Readjustment in Kentucky,* 123.

31. O. R. Vol. 16, pt. 2, 851.

Chapter 8
Confederate Plan is Laid to Destroy 7th Division

1.   O.R. Vol., 16, Pt. 2, 807.
2.   Duke, Basil W., *Reminiscences*, 312.
3.   O. R. Vol., 16, Pt. 2, 850.
4.   O. R. Vol., 16, Pt. 2, 846.
5.   Ibid, 846.
6.   Ibid, 851.
7.   Preston, John David, *The Civil War in the Big Sandy Valley of Kentucky*, (Gateway Press, Inc., Baltimore, Maryland, 1984), 60.
8.   *B & L*, Vol. I, 397.
9.   *Encyclopedia of the American Civil War*, 1255.
10. Ibid, 1255.
11. Ibid, 1255.
12. *Civil War in the Big Sandy Valley of Kentucky*, 57.
13. Ibid, 57.
14. Ibid, 65.
15. *B & L*, Vol. I, 397.
16. Ibid, 397.
17. O. R. Vol. 16, Pt. 2, 656.
18. O. R. Vol. 16, Pt. 2, 846.
19. O. R. vol. 16, Pt. 2, 870.

Chapter 9
Cumberland Gap — Fall 1862

1.   Coburn, John, *A General Recalls Civil War Experiences In Kentucky During 1861-1862*, http://kentuckexplorer.cokm/nonmembers/KEjunesampgle.html, accessed February 5, 2003.
2.   O. R. Vol. 16, (Pt. I), 993.
3.   Ibid, 993..
4.   *Cincinnati Commercial*, Vol. VXIII. No. 83, October 9, 1862.
5.   Mason, F. H., *The Forty-Second Ohio Infantry: A History*, (Cobb, Andrews & Co., Publishers, Cleveland, Ohio, 1876), 121-122.
6.   Stevenson, Benjamin F., *Letters from the Army*, (Robert Clarke & Co., Cincinnati, 1886), 119.
7.   Engle, Stephen D., *Don Carlos Buell: Most Promising of All*, (The University of North Carolina   Press: Chapel Hill & London), 288

8. *Cincinnati Commercial*, Vol. VXIII. No. 83. October 9, 1862.
9. Ibid.
10. Hopkins, Owen Johnston, *Under the Flag of the Nation,* (Ohio State University Press, Columbus, Ohio, 1961).
11. *Cincinnati Commercial*, October 9, 1862.
12. O. R. Vol. 16, Pt., 1007.
13. Ibid, 1007.
14. Ibid, 1007.
15. O. R. Vol. 16, (Pt. I), 993.
16. *B & L,* Vol. III, 66.
17. Ibid, 66.
18. Speed, Thomas, *The Union Cause In Kentucky,* (The Knickerbocker Press, New York and London, 1907), 224.
19. *B & L,* Vol. III, 66.
20. Ibid, 66.
21. O. R. Vol. 16, (Pt. I), 993.
22. Ibid, 993.
23. *B & L,* Vol. III, 68.

Chapter 10
Evacuation of Cumberland Gap

1. O. R. Vol. 16 (Pt. I), 993.
2. *B & L,* Vol. III, 67.
3. Ibid, 994.
4. Ibid, 994.
5. Speed, Thomas, *Union Regiments of Kentucky,* (Union Soldiers and Sailors Monument Association, Louisville, Kentucky 1897), 688.
6. O. R. Vol. 16 (Part I), 994.
7. Stevenson, B. F., *Letters,* 119.
8. *The Memoirs of Paul Grogger – 2nd Tennessee,* http://home.cinci.rr.com/secondtennessee/grogger.htm, page 8-9 of 30, accessed Feb 16, 2003.
9. O. R. Vol. 16 (Part I), 994.
10. Hopkins, Owen Johnston, edited by Otto F. Bond, *Under the Flag of the Nation,* (Ohio State University Press, Columbus for the Ohio Historical Society, 292.
11. Ibid, 287-292.
1. Hopkins, Owen Johnston, edited by Otto F. Bond, *Under the Flag of the Nation,* (Ohio State University Press, Columbus for The Ohio

Historical Society), 37.

2. *Battles and Leaders,* Vol. III, 67.
3. Ibid, 67.
4. Ibid, 68.
5. Hopkins, *Under the Flag of the Nation,* 37.
6. Ibid, 37.
7. Ibid, 38.
8. Mason, William Franklin, *The Journal,* page 101, private journal of Parish Brickey who was a Confederate soldier with General Humphrey. *The Journal* was written in 1954 by William Franklin Mason and transcribed by his granddaughter, Kay Mason Coutts in 1999.
20. *B & L,* 68.
21. O.R. Vol. 16, (Part I), 994
22. O.R. Vol. 16, (Part I), 994
23. O.R. Vol. 16, (Part I), 994
24. Ibid, 994
25. Hopkins, *Under the Flag of the Nation,* 38.
26. Ibid, 38.
27. Ibid, 38-39.
28. O.R. Vol. 16, (Part I), 994.
29. *The Memoirs of Paul Grogger,* 9.
30. Headley, J. T., *The Great Rebellion,* (American Publishing Company, Hartford, Conn. 1866), 108.
31. O.R., Vol. 16, (Part II), 850.
32. *The Memoirs of Paul Grogger,* 9.
33. Ibid, 9.
34. *Cincinnati Daily Gazette,* October 6, 1862, Vol. 74, No. 85.
35. O.R., Vol. 16, (Part II), 994.
36. *The Memoirs of Paul Grogger,* 9.
37. O. R. Vol. 16,(Part II), 994.
38. Ibid, 994.
39. Stevenson, B. F., *Letters,* 120; Mason, F. H., *The Forty-Second Ohio Infantry: a History,* (Cobb, Andrews & Co., Publishers, Cleveland 1876), 126.
40. Ibid, 120.
41. Ibid, 120.
42. Ibid, 120.
43. O. R. Vol. 16, (Part I), 995.
44. Ibid, 995.

Chapter 11
Confederate Pursuit

1. O. R. Vol. 16 (Part I), 1010
2. O. R. Vol. 16 (Part II), 873.
3. O. R. Vol. 16 (Part I), 1010.
4. *The Memoirs of Paul Grogger,* 9.
5. Civil War Times Illustrated, Oct 1985, Vol. XXIV, No.6, *Morgan n the Mountains* by James M. Prichard.
6. Commager, Henry Steele, *The Civil War Archive: The History of the Civil War in Documents,* (Black Dog & Leventhal Publishers, New York, 2000), 218.
7. Duke, Basil W., *A History of Morgan's Cavalry,* (Indiana University Press, Bloomington, Indiana, 1960), 256.
8. *Morgan in the Mountains,* Prichard, 34.
9. *Morgan's Cavalry,* Duke, 256-257.

Chapter 12
Painful March to Hazel Green

1. *Cincinnati Daily Gazette,* Vol. 74, No., 88. October 9, 1862.
2. Ibid.
3. O. R. Vol. 16, (Part I), 990.
4. Ibid.
5. *Cincinnati Daily Gazette,* Vol. 74, No., 88. October 9, 1862.
6. Ibid.
7. Hopkins, Owen Johnston, *Under the Flag of the Nation,* 40.
8. Noe, Kenneth W., *Perryville,* 110.
9. Hopkins, Owen Johnston, *Under the Flag of the Nation,* 41.
10. Ibid.
11. Ibid.
12. *Cincinnati Daily Gazette,* Vol. 74, No., 88. Oct. 9, 1862.
13. Kincaid, Robert, *The Wilderness Road,* 251
14. Ibid, 252.
15. Ibid, 252.
16. Ibid, 252.
17. Hedley, J. T., *The Great Rebellion,* 112.
18. Duke, Basil W., *Morgan's Cavalry,* 257.

Chapter 13
The Road to West Liberty

1. *Cincinnati Daily Gazette,* Vol., 74, No. 85, Oct. 6, 1862
2. Ibid.
3. Duke, Basil W., *Morgan's Cavalry,* 257.
4. *Cincinnati Daily Gazette,* Vol., 74, No. 85, Oct. 6, 1862.
5. O. R. Vol. 16 (Part I), 995.
6. *Cincinnati Daily Gazette,* Vol., 74, No. 85, Oct. 6, 1862.
7. Ibid.
8. Hopkins, Owen Johnston, *Under the Flag of the Nation,* 41.
9. *Cincinnati Daily Gazette,* Vol., 74. No. 85, Oct.6, 1862.
10. Duke, Basil W., *Morgan's Cavalry,* 257.
11. *Cincinnati Daily Gazette,* Oct.6, 1862.
12. Duke, Basil W., *Morgan's Cavalry,* 257.
13. *Cincinnati Daily Gazette,* Oct, 1862.
14. Ibid.
15. Duke, Basil W., *Morgan's Cavalry,* 257-258.
16. Ibid, 258.
17. Ibid, 258.
18. Ibid, 258.
19. *Cincinnati Daily Gazette,* Oct. 6, 1862.
20. *The Memoirs of Paul Grogger,* 9.
21. *Cincinnati Daily Gazette,* Oct. 6, 1862.
22. O. R. Vol. 16, (Part I), 995.
23. *The Memoirs of Paul Grogger,* 9.
24. *Cincinnati Daily Gazette,* Oct. 6, 1962.
25. Duke, Basil W., *Morgan's Cavalry,* 258.
26. O. R. Vol. 16, (Part I), 995.
27. Personal War Record of Brigadier General Richard Montgomery Gano (Unpublished) 1910. (Morgan's Mountain Campaign)
28. Duke, Basil W., *Morgan's Cavalry,* 259.

Chapter 14
Where is Humphrey Marshall?

1. O. R. Vol. 16, (Part II), 851
2. O. R. Vol. 16, (Part II), 865.
3. O. R. Vol. 16, (Part II), 866.

4. O. R. Vol. 16, (Part II), 867.
5. O. R. Vol. 16, (Part II), 870.
6. O. R. Vol. 16, (Part II), 873.
7. Guerrant, Edward O., *Bluegrass Confederate,* (Louisiana State University Press, Baton Rouge, 1999), 151. (Edited by William c. Davis and Meredith L. Swentor)
8. Ibid, 151.
9. Ibid, 152.
10. Gano, Richard Montgomery, Vol. I, *Morgan's Mountain Campaign in Eastern Kentucky,* (Unpublished notes, 1910.)
11. Guerrant, *Bluegrass Confederate,* 153.
12. O. R. Vol. 16, (Part II), 859.
13. O. R. Vol. 16, (Part II), 871.
14. Mason, William Franklin, *The Journal,* Private notes of Confederate soldier, Parish Brickey, who was a soldier in General Humphrey Marshall's army. *The Journal* was written in 1954 by William Franklin Mason and transcribed by his granddaughter, Kay Mason Coutts in 1999.
15. Engle, Stephen D., *Don Carlos Buell,* 290.
16. O. R. Vol. 16, (Part II), 870.
17. O. R. Vol. 16, (Part II), 870.
18. O. R. Vol. 16, (Part II), 556.
19. Guerrant, *Bluegrass Confederate,* 152.

Chapter 15
The Road to Grayson

1. *The Memoirs of Paul Grogger,* 9.
2. Stacy, Helen Price and Nickell, William Lynn, *Selections from Morgan County History,* (www.EWDesigns.com/nickell, 1972), 132.
3. Ibid, 167.
4. Ibid, 311.
5. Mason, F. H., *The Forty-Second Ohio Infantry,* (Cobb, Andrews & Co., Cleveland, Ohio 1876.), 133.
6. "Morgan in the Mountains", *Civil War Times Illustrated,* (October 1985, pp. 32-37).
7. Nickell, Joe, *Raids & Skirmishes: The Civil War in Morgan,* (Nickell Genealogical Books, West Liberty, Kentucky, 1991), 10.
8. *Cincinnati Daily Gazette,* Vol. 74, No. 85, October 6, 1862.

9. *The Memoirs of Paul Grogger,* 9.

10. *Cincinnati Daily Gazette,* Vol. 74, No. 85, October 6, 1862.

11. Ibid.

12. Ibid.

13. Ibid.

14. Ibid.

15. Ibid.

16. Ibid.

17. Ibid.

18. Prichard, James M., *Morgan in the Mountains,* Civil War Times Illustrated, Vol. XXIV, No. 6, (Oct 1985).

19. Duke, Basil W., *Morgan's Cavalry,* 259.

20. O. R. Vol. 16 (Part I), 995.

21. Duke, Basil W., *Morgan's Cavalry,* 259.

22. Ibid, 259.

23. Stewart, Judge John Frew, *The Last Statement of Judge John Frew Stewart,* Pikeville College's Allara Library Special Collections Room, Pikeville, Kentucky; http://www.geocities.com/eastkentuckypapers/jfs09.html, accessed April 13, 2003.

24. Speed, *Union Regiments of Kentucky,* 504.

25. Speed, Thomas, *The Union Case in Kentucky 1860-1865,* (G.P. Putnam's Sons, New York and London, The Knickerbocker Press, 1907), 224.

26. Ibid.

27. *Cincinnati Commercial,* Vol. VXIII, No. 83, Oct. 9, 1862.

28. Grogger, Paul, *Memoirs,* 10.

29. Mason, F.H., *The Forty-Second Ohio Infantry,* (Cobb, Andrews & Co. Cleveland, Ohio 1876), 134.

30. Reid, William Warner, *Diary,* Company C. 16th Ohio Infantry, 7, http://www.mkwe.com/ohio/pages/Reid-01.htm, accessed on Jan 19, 2004.

31. *Ashland Daily Independent,* Ashland, Kentucky, Oct. 5, 1958.

32. Stewart, Earl H., *The Kentucky Explorer,* September, 1999.

33. *Ashland Daily Independent,* Ashland, Kentucky, Oct. 5, 1958.

34. *Ashland Daily Independent,* Ashland, Kentucky, Sept. 13, 1959

35. Duke, *Morgan's Cavalry,* 259-260.

36. *Cincinnati Daily Gazette,* Vol. 74, No. 85, October 6, 1862.

37. Ibid.

38. Reid, William Warner, *Dairy,* 7.

39. *Cincinnati Daily Gazette,* Vol. 74, No. 85, October 6, 1862.

40. Mason, F.H., *The Forty-Second Ohio Infantry,* (Cobb, Andrews & Co., Cleveland, Oho 1876), 135-136.

41. Reid, William Warner, *Dairy*, 7.
42. Duke, *Morgan's Cavalry*, 259.

Chapter 16
The Road to Greenup

1. Reid, William Warner, *Diary*, 7.; *Cincinnati Daily Gazette*, Vol. No. 85, October 6, 1862.
2. *Cincinnati Daily Gazette*, Vol. 74. No. 85, October 6, 1862.
3. Rizk, Estelle S., *No more Muffled Hoof Beats*, (Dorrance & Company, Philadelphia), 14.
4. Ibid, 14.
5. Ibid. 15-16.
6. Interview with Mr. George Easterling at his residence located in Oldtown, Kentucky on September 8, 2003.
7. Ibid.
8. *Cincinnati Daily Gazette*, Vol. 74, No. 85, October 6, 1862.
9. Ibid.
10. Reid, William Warner, *Diary*, 7.
11. *Cincinnati Daily Gazette*, Vol. 74, No. 85, October 6, 1862.
12. Ibid.
13. Mason, F. H., *The Forty-Second Ohio Infantry*, (Cobb, Andrews & Co., Cleveland, Ohio 1876), 136-136.
14. Mason, F. H., *The Forty-Second Ohio Infantry*, (Cobb, Andrews & Co., Cleveland, Ohio 1876), 136.
15. *Cincinnati Daily Gazette*, Vol. 74, No. 85, October 6, 1862.
16. Headley, J. T., *the Great Rebellion, Vol. II*, 113.
17. *Cincinnati Daily Gazette*, Vol. 74, No. 85, October 6, 1862.
18. Hopkins, Owen Johnston, *Under the Flag of the Nation*, 42.
19. Ibid, 42.
20. Reid, William Warner, *Diary*, 7.
21. *Cincinnati Daily Gazette*, Vol. 74, No. 85, October 6, 1862.
22. Ibid.
23. Ibid.
24. Reid, William Warner, *Diary*, 7.
25. *Cincinnati Daily Gazette*, Vol. 74, No. 85, October 6, 1862.
26. Speed, *Union Regiments of Kentucky*, 504.
27. Hopkins, Owen Johnston, *Under the Flag of the Nation*, 42.
28. *Cincinnati Daily Gazette*, Vol. 74, No.88, October 9, 1862.
29. Ibid.
30. O. R. Vol. 16 (Part I), 995.

31. Reid, William Warner, *Diary*, 7.
32. Ibid.
33. Mason, F.H., *the Forty-Second Ohio Infantry*, (Cobb, Andrews & Co., Cleveland, Ohio 1876), 137.

Chapter 17
Principles of War & Morgan's Leadership Skills

1. Matloff, Maurice (General Editor), *American Military History*, (U.S. Government Printing Office, 1968), 5.
2. Ibid, 6-7.
3. Morgan, *Report*, 6.
4. Ibid, 6.
5. Ibid, 6.
6. Ibid, 6.
7. Blanchard, Kenneth, *The One Minute Manager*, (Berkley Books, New York) 1982.
8. Morgan, *Report*, 5.
9. Ibid, 6.
10. Ibid, 5.
11. O.R. Series 1 — Vol. 16 (Part I), page 990.

Chapter 18
Epilogue

1. Engle, Stephen D., *Don Carlos Buell: Most Promising of All*, (The University of North Carolina Press: Chapel Hill & London, 1999), 314.
2. Ibid, 323.
3. Ibid, 323.
4. Ibid, 333.
5. Ibid, 333.
6. Ibid, 333.
7. Garrison, Webb, *Civil War Curiosities*, (Rutledge Hill Press, Nashville, Tennessee, 1994), 97.
8. O. R. Vol. 16 (Part I), 1103.
9. *Don Carlos Buell*, 282.
10. O. R. Vol. 16 (Part I), 990.
11. O. R. Vol. 16 (Part I), 1002.

12. O. R. Vol. 16 (Part I), 1003.
13. O. R. Vol. 16 (Part I), 1005.
14. Ironton Ohio Register newspaper, October 23, 1862.
15. Headley, J. T., *The Great Rebellion*, Vol. II, 113-114.
16. Hopkins, Owen Johnston, *Under the Flag of the Nation*, 36.
17. Mason, F. H., *The Forty-Second Ohio Infantry*, (Cobb, Andrews & Co., Cleveland, Ohio, 1876), 138.
18. Ibid, 138-139.
19. James, Artus, *The Kentucky Mountains During the Civil War*; a Dissertation submitted to the Faculty of the Graduate School of Arts and Sciences, in Partial Fulfillment of the Requirements of the Degree of MA, University of Louisville,(1926), 60.
20. Stevenson, B. F., *Letters From the Army*, (Robert Clarke & Co., Cincinnati, 1886), 125.
21. Ibid, 127.